LOGAN PEARSALL SMITH

LOGAN PEARSALL SMITH

An anthology

EDITED BY
EDWARD BURMAN

Constable · London

First published in Great Britain 1989
by Constable and Company Limited
10 Orange Street London WC2H 7EG
Extracts from the work of Logan Pearsall Smith,
copyright © The Estate of Logan Pearsall Smith
Introduction and text, copyright © Edward Burman
Set in Linotron Sabon 11pt by
Rowland Phototypesetting Limited
Bury St Edmunds, Suffolk
Printed in Great Britain by
St Edmundsbury Press Limited
Bury St Edmunds, Suffolk

British Library CIP data
Smith, Logan Pearsall
An anthology
I. Title   II. Burman, Edward
818'.5209

ISBN 0 09 468530 4

CONTENTS

5

CONTENTS

EDITOR'S NOTE

L OGAN PEARSALL SMITH was both a fine writer and an important
literary influence in Britain for several decades. As a critic, his
careful scholarship produced essays which were widely praised
and influential – especially those in the volume *Words and Idioms*. His
small book on Shakespeare, although often derided by academic
critics, contains many fine observations on Shakespeare's language
and characterization.

His literary fictions, modelled on Flaubert and Baudelaire, were very
much *sui generis* and cannot readily be placed into the usual literary
categories. They are slight, and he never pretended them to be
otherwise. But they too are full of fine observation, an extremely finely
honed irony and superb control of English prose.

For many years Logan Pearsall Smith lived in a privileged position
on the edge of the British literary world. Already well-connected
through family friendships with such writers as Walt Whitman,
William and Henry James, he became related to Bernard Berenson and
Bertrand Russell through his sisters' marriages. The list of his friends,
acquaintances and correspondents is so extensive that it would be
quite possible to create a fresh and original view of English literary life
in the early years of this century from a close study of his life.

Yet little of his work is in print, and much of it has never been
reprinted since the 1930s. Some of his critical thought and linguistic
research is extremely dated and does not perhaps warrant republication except on purely academic grounds. And many of the fictions
seem quaint and slightly absurd to a modern reader. His production
was not great: he himself refers with delicate irony in the Preface to
Trivia to his practice of polishing prose until there was almost nothing
left. Thus he is a particularly suitable candidate for an anthology
which can provide the essence of his personality, critical interest and
achievement in 'fiction' in a single volume.

The anthology has been divided into three parts: 1. passages from Logan Pearsall Smith's autobiography; 2. criticism; 3. fictions.

The autobiography, *Unforgotten Years* (1938), is a fine piece of craftsmanship which provides the best possible introduction to the unusual personality of this reclusive and private man. The passages chosen are designed to illustrate three principal aspects of the man and writer: his original motivation to write and study, the highly developed sense of irony which was perhaps his main weapon both in developing defensive strategies in everyday life and in his writing, and the enthusiasm for literary research which emanates from his own account of manuscript hunting. The precise aim in selecting these passages has been to enhance enjoyment and understanding of the selections in the next two parts of the anthology.

The most important and interesting criticism is contained in *Words and Idioms* (1925) and *On Reading Shakespeare* (1933). Nearly half the former volume is taken up by the essay on English idioms, which, although interesting, is dated and also contains numerous lists which make it unsuitable for republication in an anthology such as this. Of the other essays, 'English Sea Terms' is of quite specialized interest while 'English Words Abroad', although original in its perspective, is perhaps the least satisfactory essay in the book. It seems to me that the most important and durable essay is 'Four Romantic Words', which can still be read with both interest and profit.

Similarly, his assault on the academic critics of Shakespeare can still be read with some interest – and perhaps amusement. His refusal to see the sonnet 'problem' as a problem and his exhortation to read and enjoy the poems are exemplary. The passages chosen from *On Reading Shakespeare* are intended to illustrate Pearsall Smith's fine ear for language and his role in the critical debate of the 1920s and 1930s on the question of whether Shakespeare can be 'read' or must necessarily be performed in the theatre.

While the above selections can be justified with relative ease, the choices from the fictions are much more subjective. An attempt has been made to choose those fictions which are most successful within their own terms or which show Pearsall Smith's irony at its best. But this part of the anthology is necessarily a matter of personal taste, based upon many years of reading and rereading them.

It is hoped that the above selection of passages from his work will be representative of his writings, and together with the Introduction form a useful function in bringing the writing of this long-out-of-print author to a new readership.

INTRODUCTION

LOGAN PEARSALL SMITH's brief obituary in *The Times*, on 4 March 1946, stated that his two volumes of short fictions *Trivia* and *More Trivia* were 'original masterpieces in a convention which he had created for himself'. It is probably this idiosyncrasy, and the fact that he did not work within a recognized literary genre, which prevent his work being better known today. If he is remembered, it is for his essays on the English language or his slim volume on Shakespeare.

Yet his work does bear rereading and has much to instruct us. His aims were never grand and within the limits he set himself his achievements were remarkable. Above all, no critic could possibly match his own self-deprecating irony. In the preface to *Trivia* he wrote:

> 'You must beware of thinking too much about style,' said my kindly adviser, 'or you will become like those fastidious people who polish and polish until there is nothing left.' 'Then there really are such people?' I asked eagerly. But the well-informed lady could give no precise information about them.
>
> I often hear of them in this tantalizing manner, and perhaps one of these days I shall have the luck to come across them.

It would be easy to dismiss Logan Pearsall Smith on the grounds of the slenderness of his literary output, and it is obvious that the kind of continuous polishing he mentions in this passage can lead to excessive preciousness. But when he succeeds the rewards are enormous; and when he applies his penetrating understanding of style to other authors or to language, the results are at least interesting and often exhilarating.

He was born into a talented and eminent Quaker family from Philadelphia, whose income derived from a glass factory in New York. Members of the family had contrived to combine success in industry and bookishness for several generations. Logan himself as a young man was acutely aware of the difference between the scholarly life of his librarian grandfather and the realization at Haverford College that 'I and my companions were simply enjoying our brief irresponsible hour in the sun, before we should take up that business career to which we were destined.' Bookishness and native tenacity won through, and many years later he was struck by the similarity of his own life to that described in his grandfather's book of memoirs, *Recollections*. His grandfather wrote:

> I believe it may safely be said that for forty years, eight hours of every day, or nearly so, have been employed in reading of the most miscellaneous character, often the best books, but too often the lighter kind.

Pearsall Smith's great-great-grandfather, James Logan, had bequeathed his books to the Philadelphia Library with the stipulation than his male descendants should be given the post of librarian. Thus it was that his grandfather became the librarian, and in fact he was succeeded by Logan's uncle – who, like his nephew much later – compiled an anthology of seventeenth-century prose.

In the maternal line, the bookishness was provided by Logan's mother, the Quaker preacher and popular religious author Hannah Whitall Smith, whose bibliography extends to fourteen titles. It was in her company that Logan first visited his country of adoption in 1872, when she made an evangelical tour of England. The family stayed at Broadlands in Hampshire, once Lord Palmerston's home and later the home of Lord Mountbatten. It had been inherited by William Cowper Temple, whose wife was a close friend of Hannah Whitall Smith and was well known as a friend and patron of the Pre-Raphaelites. In particular of Dante Gabriel Rossetti. Thus at a very early age, Logan Pearsall Smith was given a privileged introduction to English intellectual life.

Family friends in the United States included Henry and William

James, the latter being described by Logan in his autobiography as 'the most charming man I ever met'. When Logan went to Harvard, William James frequently invited the young student to dinner in his rooms. But even within the family, and through the marriages of his sisters, he was brought into contact with some of the most extraordinary people of his time. His cousin Carey Thomas was first the Dean and then President of the prestigious college Bryn Mawr. His sister Mary contributed greatly to his literary formation, returning regularly from her studies at Smith College with news of the latest ideas and literary fashions. As the result of one such enthusiasm, Walt Whitman was invited to dinner during the summer vacation of 1882. The evening was such a success that Whitman – invited for a single evening – stayed with the generous and hospitable Pearsall Smiths for an entire month.

One of the most fascinating, and as yet unresearched, aspects of Logan Pearsall Smith's purely literary influence is that on his brothers-in-law. Their eminence even at that time and the fact that they chose Pearsall Smiths for their brides give us some indication both of the intellectual life and of the openness of the entire family.

The second husband of his beloved sister Mary was Bernard Berenson, while Alys achieved even higher intellectual and social status in marrying Bertrand Russell. There is ample evidence that both Berenson and Russell were influenced considerably by their young brother-in-law and master of style. Logan assisted Berenson in the writing and editing of his early books on art history, and in fact his own first published work was published privately while Logan was resident with Berenson in Tuscany. More interesting, in view of the elegance of his style and persuasiveness of his less philosophical and more political works, was the influence on Bertrand Russell. In a letter written to Ottoline Morrell on 15 April 1912, Russell wrote that 'when I was young, [Logan] had a very good influence on me'.

With such a background, we may well imagine the depression suffered by Logan Pearsall Smith – after listening to Jowett at his sister's wedding breakfast at Balliol, after meeting Matthew Arnold in Dresden in 1885, and after hearing Edmund Gosse lecture at Harvard – when he was sent to work in the offices of the family business in New York. But although such an experience may have dampened the literary enthusiasm of a less-determined man, he worked secretly on his first short story. It was published in the New York *Evening Post* in 1886. In his own words, it was writing which sustained him through the boredom of business:

> ... these stolen secret joys, this foretaste of what has been since the delight and torture of my life, made me turn away with more persistence from the den of business ... Outside was Europe, and golden leisure, long tranquil days of writing.

Logan was fortunate in having an understanding and generous father. He was given the choice between a regular allowance to do as he wished and a sum of $25,000 in cash to buy himself an annuity. He chose the latter, and left the United States to study in Oxford and then live in England for the rest of his life. In 1913 he took British nationality, and in fact only returned to his native land once after this departure in 1888 – for an operation at the Johns Hopkins Hospital in Baltimore thirty-three years later.

At Oxford, he entered the privileged society of Benjamin Jowett, Master of Balliol, which provided him with what he refers to as 'some elements of real education'. His acquaintances included Lawrence Binyon and Max Beerbohm, while he was influenced stylistically by Walter Pater. His taste was refined by this Oxford residence, and he began a collection of paintings with some oils by William Blake. His main friendships at Balliol were with members of great Whig families like the Russells, Peels and Howards, and he became actively involved in canvassing for the Liberal party.

Perhaps the most formative experience of those years, especially for his own creative work, was, however, a period spent in Paris in 1891. Once again, literary friendships were important: his Paris friends included Walter Raleigh, Lowes Dickinson and Roger Fry. The latter became a particularly close friend, and it was through him that Pearsall Smith later met the American painter James McNeill Whistler, and sat for him while he painted his celebrated portrait of Comte Robert de Montesquieu which was exhibited at the 1894 Salon, and is now part of the Frick Collection in New York. Although Denys Sutton, in his study of Whistler (Phaidon, 1966) states that this portrait was painted in London, Pearsall Smith recalls sitting for it in Paris. He describes the scene with typical irony: 'I was, like him, tall and slim, and could competently stand there with what was the principal feature of the picture, the fur coat flung across the arm.'

But the most significant discoveries of this Paris period were the novels and letters of Flaubert and the stories of Flaubert's nephew Guy de Maupassant. He may also have made his first acquaintance with the poetry and prose fictions of Baudelaire during this Paris residence, although he himself attributes this discovery to a moment of insight into the potential of Baudelaire's prose paragraphs which occurred in his Sussex home four years later. They were later to become the major direct influence on his own fictions. But Flaubert was to be a constant presence in Logan Pearsall Smith's writing career.

Fifty years later, he wrote with regard to the impact of Flaubert on his style:

> . . . and now, when I look again at the texts I marked, the old flames illuminate those pages. The true writer is a kind of priest, he says, his devotion makes him proud, and we are none of us proud enough. 'But when I think of my solitude and my agonies I ask myself whether I am an idiot or a saint. But without fanaticism we can accomplish nothing worthwhile, and folly for folly why not choose the noblest among them?
>
> 'Genius is a gift of the Gods, but Talent is our affair; and with untiring patience one can acquire talent in the end. But why should one publish? I write for my own pleasure, as a bourgeois in his garret turns out napkin rings on his lathe . . . The wine of art is the cause of an intoxication that knows no end . . . Speaking with all sincerity everything is ignominy here below but art.'
>
> These are some of the sentences I copied out from Flaubert's letters. I believed them all. (And, idiotic as it may seem, I still believe them).

The elegant and self-deprecating parenthesis is typical of Logan Pearsall Smith, and here serves to disarm possible accusations of aestheticism. The lesson of Flaubert was exemplary. Few authors in the English language have possessed such a perfect sense of pitch, and such control of each word and cadence. One quick check-list of these authors could in fact be compiled by the simple method of looking at the index to Pearsall Smith's own anthology, the *Treasury of English Prose* (1919). His selections from the prose of the St James version of the Bible, John Donne, Sir Thomas Browne and Jeremy Taylor illustrate the excellence of his judgement. They also, incidentally, provide evidence of a taste which anticipated new trends – particularly in the case of Donne.

In 1895 he published a small volume of short stories about Oxford, entitled *The Youth of Parnassus*, on which he had started working during his Paris sojourn. Looking back at this early work he referred to it as a 'laboured, imitative, rather lifeless book' which 'of course fell completely flat'. But it did serve a useful function in bringing him the friendship of Robert Bridges, which was to last until Bridges died in 1930. A copy had also been sent to Henry James, who lost it on the London Underground; on being sent a second copy, James invited Pearsall Smith to visit him and discuss the stories. But the novelist was not enthusiastic: 'His praise was kind but tepid: I think he saw the gift for story telling was not my gift.' He impressed on the younger man the importance of loneliness for the writer, a suggestion which resolved a pressing problem. For Logan Pearsall Smith's income would not have been sufficient for him to live well in London, while he could live a quiet and comfortable life in the country.

It was thus that he took the rented house called High Buildings in Sussex, not far from a larger house which his father rented. This house was to be his home for the next ten years, and the period of intensive study which he embarked upon in the Sussex countryside was to form the basis of his literary output for the rest of his life. In 1914 he moved to a house at St Leonard's Terrace in Chelsea with his sister Alys. They remained there together until Logan's death in 1948.

His time at High Buildings was totally devoted to reading and copying out favourite quotations for later anthologies. He once wrote that, 'I have always been fond of anthologising. I think it a dainty occupation for a person of leisure and literary taste.' We are provided with a vivid glimpse of this life-long habit of collecting quotations by Virginia Woolf's diary entry for Sunday, 18 May 1919. It also gives us a rare description of his conversational brilliance and unusual personality:

> . . . then Logan came; and we only fell silent at half past six or even later; nor was there a moment of repose, neither for tongue nor brain. It is true that Logan does his turns, which take the form of 'delightful adventures – life is like the Arabian Nights –' & good stories, quotations, & recitations; but even these require intelligent attention. He is a very well brushed, bright eyed, rosy cheeked man, seemingly entirely satisfied with life, which he appears to have mastered; visiting each of its flowers, like a bee. These flowers he keeps stored in his waistcoat pocket: lines from Jeremy Taylor, Carlyle, Lamb &c.

That was in fact the year of publication of his *Treasury of English Prose*.

Logan Pearsall Smith's book of Shakespeare criticism is fascinating, among other things, for the unexpected gems of poetry which he seems to pluck out from corners of the plays left untouched by the critics. His insistence on the *poetry* of Shakespeare's plays informs his criticism and is at the heart of his fundamental disagreement with the academic critics: his main target was in fact the emphasis placed upon historical background in the work of the American scholar E. E. Stoll – whom he refers to as 'the Sphinx' or 'the Monster of the Middle West'.

But this critical work also provides important insights into his own creative writing. In the fourth chapter of *On Reading Shakespeare* he describes how after the early plays an odd thing happens on the stage:

> Now and then, among the attendants of the great stage dummies, a humble figure comes to life; an eye catches our eye, we hear the sound of a living voice, and the sense of the theatre is replaced for a moment by the illusion of reality. These real people appear first in scenes which are, for the most part, of no importance; they are but embryos and are presented sketchily at first, like Launce and Speed, in the *Two Gentlemen of Verona*, and the Host in that play, who, hiding with Julia as she woefully listens to her false

lover declare his love to her rival, suddenly awakes with the exclamation: 'By my halidom, I was fast asleep.'

He goes on to show how this process continues with Bottom, Juliet's nurse and other minor characters. But, apart from the interest of the observation, this criticism indicates a particular perception of the author since he builds his own fictions around these unexpected colloquialisms that suddenly bring a character to life. He goes on to state that 'when Shakespeare makes them speak or act, as he sometimes does, out of these inferred, but unportrayed aspects of their nature, he produces an astonishing effect of unforeseen, yet inevitable, reality and truth.'

It is exactly that 'unforeseen reality and truth' which he tries to encapsulate in his fictions by turning an apparently obvious remark into something surprising or unexpected – always tinged by the melancholy irony of the author. A character is sketched in a few brief utterances, or, even more effectively, the narrator reveals a hitherto unknown aspect of his own character. For example, in *Waxworks*.

Although Cyril Connolly, who for a period worked as amanuensis to Logan Pearsall Smith, described him in *Enemies of Promise* as 'one of the last of the old Mandarins', his ear for both prose and poetry was excellent. It is true that he does often lapse into Mandarin prose, which Connolly defined as characterized by 'long sentences with many dependent clauses, by the use of the subjunctive and conditional, by exclamations and interjections, quotations, allusions, metaphors, long images, Latin terminology, subtlety and conceits'. But he provides excellent advice when he recommends prospective dramatists to 'study above all the speech rhythms, the syntax, the hesitations, the tricks of phrase and verbal sing-song' of the people with whom he talks. And it is difficult not to forgive Pearsall Smith his lapses into Mandarin when he writes of his delight in seeing 'some ancient, primitive word appear with its face washed and its eyes shining', or directs us straight to some of the minor but telling utterances of Shakespeare's characters.

This artisan-like care and interest in the English language led him to make a close study of the *Oxford English Dictionary* then gradually appearing. One of his ambitions was in fact to introduce a new word into that dictionary: he never succeeded but always hoped that his coinage 'milver', roughly synonymous with amanuensis, would make it. As the result of these researches he published *The English Language* for the Home University Library in 1912 and the more important *Words and Idioms* – subtitled 'Studies in the English Language' – in 1925. He also wrote pamphlets for the Society of Pure English.

The English Language is a straightforward history of the language based upon scholarly works by Skeat, Sayce, Sweet and Jespersen. The author himself tells us in the Preface that it is especially based on Bradley's *The Making of English*. *Words and Idioms* is more original both in conception and in the research, and marks a new kind of literary scholarship which was impossible before the publication of the Oxford dictionary. It is divided into five essays: 'English Sea Terms', 'The English Element in Foreign Languages', 'Four Romantic Words', 'Popular Speech and Standard English', and 'English Idioms'. The third essay is of particular interest, and a precursor of modern critical method in its use of the historical evidence provided by the Oxford dictionary. In it he argues that 'a cluster of new terms, or of old terms endowed with new meanings' can be studied in such a way as to define the beginning of the Romantic movement. He chooses the words 'romantic', 'originality', 'creation', and 'genius', and illustrates the shift of meaning which they undergo in English and other European languages in the process of becoming defining characteristics of Romanticism.

In a lifetime of literary research and library visiting, Logan Pearsall Smith also made several minor discoveries. One of the most interesting was his location of four important letters written by John Donne. They were published by the Donne scholar, Herbert Grierson, and incorporated in John Hayward's Nonesuch *Complete Poetry and Selected Prose* (1929). He also discovered letters of Walpole and Carlyle.

It was this care and craftsmanship, together with constant reading and rereading of the great authors, which led Logan Pearsall Smith to the finely honed perfection of the literary credo which he attempted to put into practice in his own short fictions.

In his solitude at High Buildings in the closing years of the nineteenth century, he was absorbed by the idea of exploiting the paragraph or page further than had been done before. The point of departure was to be that of Baudelaire's *Journaux Intimes*: 'Something like Baudelaire in style was what I dreamed of; but a style more idiomatic, more colloquial, yet capable of rising to the heights of English prose.'

It was an ambitious project which entailed encapsulating a particular moment, idea or phrase in a short piece of heightened prose. Pearsall Smith himself provided the best statement of what he was attempting to do in his autobiography. The passage is worth quoting in full as his clearest explanation of the idea behind his prose fictions:

> But what was it exactly that wanted to find expression in the little book I meditated? They were not things that lay on the surface of consciousness, ready to be put into words. The world is full of conscious thoughts, which have found adequate expression; but I was haunted now and then by intimations which seemed to have a significance which I could not understand. The things that seemed to want to be said were latent meanings which no one had yet put into words; which would have to find the words themselves for their expression. In a sentence I overheard in conversation, or in something which, often to my surprise, I would hear myself saying, or in the memory of an exultation or humiliation or grotesque encounter, there would seem to lie a meaning, an ironic, grotesque, perhaps a profound significance. I became more and more haunted by a sense of the oddity of existence, of the fact that, as Plato hinted, this universe is not one which should be taken too seriously, or that our personal affairs were not worthy, as he said, of the care and anxiety that the ignominy of existence forced us to bestow upon them.

This sense of oddity, sustained by a finely developed irony, is the most obvious quality of his fictions. Several of the fictions in *Trivia* and *More Trivia*, included in this selection, turn on a conclusion which surprises the reader and often the narrator. Others are based upon snatches of conversation. At their best, these short fictions are superb evocations and – once we have emphasized their slightness and the innate modesty of their author – may rank with some of the finest prose writing of the twentieth century.

Quite often, in these oblique glimpses of the social world built upon a single phrase of overheard conversation, Pearsall Smith reminds us of the technique of Ronald Firbank. Each writer achieves intense effects by skilful use of indirect irony and a technique for constructing dialogue which resembles montage. An excellent example of this can be seen in the fiction At the Club, where a series of apparently random assertions provide a review of the typical prejudices of the members of a gentleman's club, as perceived by Pearsall Smith. This montage is brought to a close by the perfect *reductio ad absurdum* of his ironic persona, as the narrator adds a comment which is obviously ridiculous, even at first sight, but on reflection no more ridiculous than the other affirmations. This appears to be an improvement on Firbank's technique. But in fact Firbank's first published novel was *Vainglory* (1915), three years before the publication of *Trivia* by Constable but thirteen years after the first publication of many of the fictions. In the intervening years, some had also been published by Desmond MacCarthy in the *New Statesman*. The matter of literary influence is not as straightforward as it appears, and it would be interesting to study this technique as it was developed by Firbank and later by Evelyn Waugh.

We have seen how Pearsall Smith himself attributed the original idea to his reading of Baudelaire's prose paragraphs, and it is possible to discern several instances of direct influence. This sentence in *Fusées VI*, for example, 'Les méprises relatives aux visages sont le résultat de l'éclipse de l'image réelle par l'hallucination qui en tire sa naissance,' leads to a typically Pearsall Smith vision on a London bus:

> As I sat inside that crowded bus, so sad, so incredible and sordid seemed the fat face of the woman opposite me, that I interposed the thought of Kilamanjaro, that highest mountain of Africa, between us . . .

The persona which he developed wanders through London, by bus or on foot, listening and observing, dining with the Vicar, talking to old ladies at dinner parties, constantly on the look-out for the oddities of life and reporting them in exquisite prose as if he were a modest but realistic philosopher.

Two other aspects of Baudelaire's work are transplanted directly into the fictions. First, the personification of everyday objects, as in this passage from *Fusées VIII*:

> Ces beaux et grands navires, imperceptiblement balancés (dandinés) sur les eaux tranquilles, ces robustes navires, à l'air désoeuvré et nostalgique, ne nous disent-ils pas dans une langue muette: Quand partons-nous pour le bonheur?

Second, what may be described as a kind of pure, philosphical Mandarin, as in this part of Section XXX of *Mon Coeur mis à nu*:

> Pourquoi le spectacle de la mer est-il si infinement et si éternelle-ment agréable?
> Parce que la mer offre à la fois l'idée de l'immensité et du movement. Six ou sept lieues représentent pour l'homme le rayon de l'infini. Voilà un infini diminutif. Qu'importe s'il suffit à suggérer l'idée de l'infini total? Douze ou quatorze lieues (sur le diamètre), douze ou quatorze de liquide en mouvement suffisent pour donner la plus haute idée de beauté qui soit offerte à l'homme sur son habitacle transitoire.

It is interesting to observe both these aspects in the first fiction of *Trivia*, entitled 'Happiness'. In that fiction the same connection is made between happiness and the ships setting sail. But even more important is the essential notion that what happiness we are likely to find can in fact be found in the small space that we inhabit, and in the familiar objects that surround us. In short, in trivia.

The quality in these fictions which prevents them slipping into banality is Pearsall Smith's keen sense of irony, instilled into the modest persona created as the narrator of the fictions. A strong sense of irony was often noticed by his friends, and the fact that he was extremely conscious of it is suggested by references to 'my love of irony' in his autobiography. In an entry in his journal for 10 August 1896 he wrote: 'I dreamt last night that the Lord appeared to me, and the Lord spake and said, "The only way to treat modern life is the ironic – you cannot make it romantic."'

An example of irony used against himself, and redeeming an otherwise over-purple passage, may be found in the fiction 'The Poplar', in *More Trivia*. The control of the prose in this fiction demonstrates how his sense of irony is sufficient to save him both from banal philosophizing and from the excesses of Mandarin sentimentality. It is given here in full:

> There is a great tree in Sussex, whose cloud of thin foliage floats high in the summer air. The thrush sings in that umbrage, and blackbirds, who fill the late, decorative sunshine with a shimmer of golden sound. There the nightingale finds her green cloister; and on those branches sometimes, like a great fruit, hangs the lemon-coloured Moon. In the glare of August, when all the world is faint with heat, there is always a breeze in those cool recesses; always a noise, like the noise of water, among their lightly hung leaves.
>
> But the owner of this Tree lives in London, reading books.

The control of pace is exemplary. After the initial straightforward proposition, 'There is a great tree in Sussex', Pearsall Smith allows himself a flourish in the subordinate clause. Then the three successive sentences grow increasingly Mandarin both in content and in syntax, drawing the reader into this detailed account of the tree. The tree is not, however, named in the text, and its attributes (the 'umbrage', the 'green cloister', the 'cool recesses' and the 'lightly-hung leaves') evoke rather than describe it.

In this way the prose is heightened into poetry, but treads the knife-edge between excellence and over-writing. It is typical of Logan Pearsall Smith, and his control, that he is able to bring the whole structure back to earth again. This feat is managed by the last sentence, with its deliberate self-deprecation. Like an expert horseman he knows when to let out the reins, and precisely how much they can be let out. Then, when it is time to regain control, he is able to draw them in again in a demonstration of first-rate craftsmanship.

Such control, coupled with his fine sense of the oddity of life, his irony and his imagination, enables him to produce miniature masterpieces such as 'High Life'. Again, the point of departure is simple: the narrator has obtained an order to view a country house which is on sale. He knows from the outset that he cannot possibly afford such a vast house, but impish curiosity has pushed him to visit it in any case. The swell of the language matches the gradual bloating of the narrator's imagination as he almost convinces himself that he *could* after all buy and live in such a house. The language becomes almost over-rich. But then, exactly as in The Poplar, the whole apparatus is brought down by the astringent final paragraph. The narrator's soul has swollen to the extent that he realizes this house would never be able to contain the pride of which he is capable. He returns to his original, conversational hesitancy: 'Then for one thing there was stabling for only forty horses; and this, of course, as I told them, would never do.'

The contemporary critical stance with regard to Pearsall Smith is probably represented quite fairly by a comment made by Noel Annan in 1980 during his review of Barbara Strachey's book on his family, *Remarkable Relations*. Annan wrote that 'He was quite right in thinking that in his final collections of *Trivia* he had left a faint but indelible impression on English letters.' This is an accurate assessment, although it would be reasonable to change the order of adjectives to emphasize 'indelible' at the expense of 'faint'. Yet it excludes the wider importance of the writer through his pioneer work on language, his literary friendships and critical writing.

It is as an all-round man of letters that he deserves to be known and read today. But he is also exemplary for the lesson he can give us through the honest self-appraisal implicit in the limited quantity and consistent quality of his published writing. His creative enterprise was wisely restricted from the beginning, since such a pitch of writing cannot be sustained for long – except perhaps by such authors as his own early mentor Flaubert. The main critical problem in fact derives from the fact that his literary output was so much *sui generis* and cannot readily be placed into the usual literary categories. The derivation of the fictions from nineteenth-century French models only complicates this issue, and it is worth observing that one of the few twentieth-century writers with whose work they can be compared is also French: the Raymond Queneau of *Exercices de Style*.

In his observations on writing contained in *Unforgotten Years*, Logan Pearsall Smith refers to 'that personal rhythm, that song which in a great writer is the sound of his voice and the essence of his style'. He himself cannot be described as a great writer, and would certainly never have used such a term of his own work. But, even by his own very high standards, it may be argued that in the best of his fictions he did achieve that personal rhythm, that song.

PART I: AUTOBIOGRAPHY

from

Unforgotten Years (1938)

BOYHOOD AND YOUTH

———— ✳ ————

I T is the custom of good Americans to bestow, somewhat in the
Chinese fashion, a kind of posthumous nobility upon their ances-
tors; to transform the farmers and small tradesmen from whom
they are almost all descended into scions of great, historic English
houses. This innocent exercise of the fancy produces a good deal of
blameless satisfaction, since there is indeed, I believe, a more abiding
sense of noble birth to be derived from false than from authentic
pedigrees; and plebeian blood flows with a more consciously aristocratic thrill through the veins of those who have dyed it in the azure
of their own imaginations.

It is not for me, at least, to reprobate such delusions, for was I not
nourished in my youth upon them? Had not certain elderly and
imaginative members of my family succeeded, after long meditation,
in adorning the mediocrity of their circumstances with at least one
escutcheon, in tracing one portion of their line to aristocratic sources?

Of the plebeian lineage and name of Smith they could indeed make
little; the Smiths were only too plainly a race of Yorkshire yeoman
farmers, who, becoming Quakers, had emigrated to New Jersey in the
time of William Penn, and, settling in the quiet town of Burlington on
the Delaware, had engaged in commerce with the West Indies, watching the broad river for the arrival of small brigantines or 'snows',
which sailed thither, laden with the products of the South. But one of
them in the eighteenth century, my grandfather's grandfather, with the
respectable name of John Smith, had married a daughter of the
secretary whom William Penn had brought to Pennsylvania and left
there as his representative.

This secretary, James Logan, was, so history says, the son of a
schoolmaster of Scottish descent at Lurgan in the north of Ireland.
When the troubles of the civil war drove the family to Bristol, young
Logan was apprenticed to a linen draper, but became afterwards a

master in the school his father started there. This father belonged to a respectable Scottish family and neither he nor his son claimed a nobler derivation. In the creative imagination of their descendants in America, however, they became members of a noble and famous race, the Logans of Restalrig, and owners of that Fast Castle which was described by Scott in *The Bride of Lammermoor* as the house of Ravenswood. One of the Logans had gone to Palestine as a Crusader, to convey thither the heart of Robert Bruce, and another had been hanged, centuries later, for his participation in the Gowrie Conspiracy.

This background of crusades and crimes, with imaginary castles and gallows in the distance, shed a kind of glamour on the lives of these mild Quakers, who, in spite of the Quaker ban on worldly fiction, must, it appears, have been reading *Waverley Novels* on the sly. And was it not for them all perfectly authentic? Had not one of them crossed the Atlantic and made a special pilgrimage to Scotland, and there, on the spot, when visiting the estate of this famous family, been overcome by a profound conviction of its truth? Was not the heart of Bruce which adorned the arms of the Restalrig family (arms which James Logan had never dreamt of assuming) – was not this bleeding heart splashed upon the notepaper and engraved upon the silver of the family in Philadelphia? What genealogist could demand, what documents could provide, more convincing evidence than this?

These imagined glories rather obscured in the eyes of his descendants their ancestor's real distinction; for William Penn's secretary had become the most remarkable inhabitant of the English colonies during the first half of the eighteenth century. Remaining in Pennsylvania as the agent for William Penn and his sons, he held in turn every important office in that commonwealth. He was the master of many languages, and an authority also on mathematics and astronomy, and as a botanist he made an important contribution to the theory of the sexuality of plants. He corresponded with learned men all over Europe, and collected the finest library in America, containing all the best books on history, on art and geography, of the time, as well as all the Latin and Greek classics, including Bentley's editions. He transformed Philadelphia in fact into the Athens of America, as it was called, and it was thither that Benjamin Franklin fled in his youth from a less cultivated Boston. Of Franklin and his printing press he was one of the earliest patrons, and Franklin printed for him two of his translations from Cicero, in one of which, described as the first translation made in America from the classics, the young printer expressed a hope that 'this first translation of a classic in the Western world might be a happy omen that Philadelphia shall become the seat of the Muses'. This hope, I may note in passing, has not been yet fulfilled, though my ancestor did his best to prepare for the advent of the Nine to the Quaker city, by bequeathing his books to the Philadelphia Library which Benjamin Franklin founded there.

In the meantime his son-in-law, the John Smith I have mentioned, occupied himself in a prosperous commerce with the West Indies, exchanging grain, lumber, and other products of the North for sugar, rum, and molasses from the South. These were transported in his own vessels, built in his own shipyard at Burlington, and sailing from the wharf there which he owned. After publishing in Philadelphia, where he dwelt, a pamphlet in defence of the pacifist principles of the Quakers, he had retired to the family home at Burlington, up the river, and spent the rest of his life in reading, and, as his grandson, my grandfather, put it, in 'copying into commonplace books those senti-ments and sententious remarks of favourite authors which he approved'. This taste for copying out was shared by his family and descendants; his brother, Samuel Smith, compiled from many docu-ments a history of New Jersey which is still, I believe, cited by those who are interested in that subject; his son, who inherited the name of John Smith, inherited this taste also, and filled several volumes with the lives and memorable sayings of New Jersey Quakers; his grandson, who was my grandfather, published many colonial documents, and I too, with the various documents and anthologies I have published, have not failed in carrying on this family tradition.

I like to think of that lot of quiet and bookish old forebears, among whom was at least one minor poet, settled on the banks of the Delaware among the wigwams and papooses of the Indians, thinking their mild Quaker thoughts in their meeting-houses, or listening to the preaching of John Woolman, who also lived at Burlington, and was their friend and neighbour. They seem to have been content to spend their lives in this Quaker Arcadia, fishing in the broad river which flowed past their farms, or reading the books which trickled over to them across the Atlantic, and copying out sententious extracts from those eighteenth-century volumes.

My grandfather, however, John Jay Smith, left Burlington as a boy, and sailing down the Delaware to Philadelphia, establishing himself there first as a chemist's assistant, soon began to engage in other activities. Among the stipulations which James Logan had made in bequeathing his books to the Philadelphia Library was one to the effect that his eldest son should be the librarian, and his eldest grandson in the male line should succeed; and should the male line fail, the position should be offered to the eldest of the female line. To my grandfather this appointment was given; he occupied it many years, and was succeeded in it by one of my uncles. James Logan's will was, I believe, invalid; the position thus dubiously bequeathed was a modest one; but since it was held for more than fifty years by members of our family, our claim to this humble librarianship came to be regarded, at least by ourselves, as conferring a kind of dim distinction; and it was originally intended that I should succeed my uncle (who had no son) in this, as we imaginatively designated it, the only hereditary office in America.

It was from this old Philadelphia Library, an eighteenth-century building in the neighbourhood of Independence Square, with its air of venerable antiquity – for the few old buildings found in a new country seem to possess a more antique aspect than anything in Europe – it was in this old library, long since destroyed, with its dim interior and old folios and bewigged portraits, that I received my first bookish impressions, being often taken there as a little boy, and given a book to read by my uncle who presided over the silence of that unfrequented institution. Thus in my earliest years I became familiar with the atmosphere of old libraries, and the dim light that dwells in them, and fell under the spell which they cast upon those who haunt their precincts – that quietness, that hush of the human spirit in the ghostly presence of its own immortality, stored up in rows of ancient volumes and great folios of the classics.

But I anticipate, perhaps, my more romantic impressions of this kind. It was in this library at least that, encouraged by my librarian uncle, I first formed the habit of reading. What that habit might grow into was impressed upon me by my occasional visits to the aged ex-librarian, my grandfather, at the house to which he had retired in the Quaker suburb of Germantown, where he lived to a great old age, spending his days in his study upstairs, with his gouty toe on a cushion, reading and reading all day long. 'I believe it may be safely said,' he wrote of himself towards the end of his life, 'that for forty years, eight hours of every day, or nearly so, have been employed in reading of the most miscellaneous character, often the best books, but too often the lighter kind.' When I happened, not long ago, upon this sentence in my grandfather's *Recollections*, I was struck by the accurate description it gave of my own existence, which for the last forty years or so has been spent, like his, in miscellaneous reading, and often too, like his, 'of the lighter kind'. The analogy was a curious one; indeed, I found it more curious than pleasing; for recalling my visits to that old gentleman, I turned my eyes on my elderly self, where I sat reading upstairs, and saw myself for a disconcerting moment. And then I went on reading.

It might have increased my awe of my grandfather had I known, as I now know, that he had every right to the designation of a retired pirate, since a large portion of his earlier years had been spent in the occupation of pirating the works of famous English writers. Indeed, he has some claim to be the earliest of these pirates, since, as the *Dictionary of American Biography* states, he suggested in 1832 to Adam Waldie, a Philadelphia printer, the republication, in the absence of international copyright, of important foreign books, and became the editor of *Waldie's Select Circulating Library*, in which many English books were reprinted for American readers, without any thought of remunerating their authors. This became finally an international crime and scandal; and if I cannot boast of descent from any Scottish criminals, I may at least claim that my grandfather was the first of American literary pirates. But he incurred no blame among his contemporaries, and writes freely of these activities in his printed *Recollections*. The thing, however, which was the subject of reprobation in his lifetime, and which, reaching my ears in dark references and whispers, much increased the terror of my visits to him, was the dreadful fact that he was an 'Unbeliever'. What exactly an Unbeliever was, and what he disbelieved in, I had not the dimmest notion, but I knew that his future was thereby involved in the most dreadful consequences; and I remember a sense of the removal of an impending calamity when it was generally agreed that, by a deathbed conversion, this dark cloud had been lifted from the old gentleman's prospects in the future world.

More definite and more terrifying is the memory of one dreadful occasion when, not long before his death, my grandfather, who seldom left his study, hobbled downstairs and, establishing himself in his drawing-room, began to denounce the age, uttering sentiments of a kind that sounded incredible in my ears. The theme of his discourse – it is a theme which is familiar, perhaps too familiar, to me now – was a general castigation of the time in which he found himself, and a diatribe in especial against America, against the conditions of life and the democratic institutions of our land of freedom. Although his invective seemed to have no relation to life in America as I knew it, yet it went on for long reverberating beneath all the optimisms and enthusiasms and patriotic beliefs of my boyish years.

Thus to children at odd moments come, as through windows left unexpectedly ajar, intimations of the unknown aspects of the world they live in. In my grandfather's house there was another half-open window, through which I would sometimes peep with wondering eyes.

The life of the Quakers in Philadelphia, where we lived as children, was that of a secluded community, carefully entrenched and guarded from all contact with what we called the 'World' – that dangerous world of wickedness which, we vaguely knew, lay all about us. With that world and its guilty splendours we had no contact; of the fashionable American aristocracy (and every population has its aristocracy and fashion) we were not members; and I can make no claim, as Americans abroad are apt to claim, that I belong to one of what are called America's first families. With members of this greater world, like Edith Wharton and Mrs Winthrop Chanler, I became acquainted only after I had come to live in Europe.

No, we spent our youth amid the evangelical plainness and the simple ways of living of the stricter Philadelphia Friends. And yet, those richly carved and velvet-covered chairs which adorned my grandfather's drawing-room at Germantown, those antlers which hung on the walls of his suburban residence – these seemed to tell a tale of richer experience, and tinged for me with gay colours the past history and the European expeditions of the old gentleman who sat reading upstairs.

The Philadelphia Quakers had always kept up a connection with the members of their sect in England, and this connection was frequently renewed by the visits of English Friends on holy missions. Some of these visiting Friends belonged to the highest sphere of the Quaker world – for all religious communities, however holy, are stratified in social layers of increasing splendour – and the impressiveness of their doctrine was much augmented by a sense of the plain yet brilliant world in which they lived, a world of Barclays and Gurneys and other rich English Quaker families which, like a Quaker Versailles, holy and yet splendid, shone for us across the Atlantic with a kind of glory – a glory which, to tell the truth, has never completely faded from my eyes.

My grandfather, though not interested in their doctrines, was by no means indifferent to the country houses and opulent tables of these English Quakers; he tells of dining with Samuel Gurney at Ham House, of meeting Elizabeth Fry, and of hearing her, in her feeble but honoured old age, make a beautiful prayer from her large mahogany arm-chair in the meeting she attended. He tells also of being welcomed among a company of English Friends by a fellow Philadelphian and youthful acquaintance, Eliza P. Kirkbride, who had married, as his third wife, the eminent and opulent Joseph John Gurney.

But the great glory of this jaunt abroad of my grandfather was his visit to Stoke Park, then the residence of Granville Penn, William Penn's great-grandson and heir. Granville Penn, learning, according to my grandfather's account, – and I dare say by a note from my grandfather himself, – that a descendant of William Penn's secretary had come from Pennsylvania to England, sent him an invitation to Stoke Poges, which was accepted with alacrity. He relates how an elegant family carriage with liveried servants met him at the station; how he was conducted to the noble family mansion of the Penn family, where he spent some days, and in whose deer park he shot the buck of which the antlers afterwards adorned his suburban home; how his host drove him about the neighbourhood in a coach with four horses, and took him to Oxford, where they dined at a raised table in the hall of Christ Church, and where, he tells with undisguised elation, all the guests except Mr Penn and himself were lords.

These were indeed rich experiences; encouraged by them, my grandfather, five years after his return to America, started out on a still more glorious jaunt abroad. The great Crystal Palace Exhibition was then in preparation, and he had the happy idea of travelling to Europe as a sort of self-appointed and unofficial envoy to arrange, if possible, for the transport of this exhibition, or a portion of it, across the Atlantic after it had run its course in England. His purpose, as he states in his memoirs, was in part at least the utility to America of this plan, but his main intention, as he frankly admits, was to gain by this means 'an introduction to men of mark abroad, and a sight of foreign life behind the scenes.' Though the public part of his scheme came to no fruition, his private aim was brilliantly successful. Procuring a letter of recommendation from the Secretary of State at Washington, he proceeded to London, where he was received by Lord Granville and made the acquaintance of a certain General Gray, whom he describes as 'a most elegant and portly gentleman'. In London also he was privileged to witness the Duchess of Sutherland purchase a rug, which was indeed a sight of foreign life behind the scenes. He sat at tables, he tells his descendants, 'of the most *recherché* character'; and once when the royal box at the Opera had been lent to someone of his acquaintance, and he was invited to share it, he had reason to believe, he tells us, that he was mistaken by some of the opera-goers for a foreign prince who was then on a visit to England.

My grandfather had married a Rachel Pearsall, of a Quaker family in Long Island, and my father, Robert Pearsall Smith, was, by his marriage in 1851 to my mother, Hannah Whitall, introduced into surroundings and circumstances different from those of his own family. His wife's father, John Whitall, was descended from another, more pious and less bookish line of New Jersey Quakers, being the grandson of that rather terrific Ann Whitall, of whose old religious journal I have written elsewhere. He had run away to sea as a boy, and, sailing before the mast on East Indian voyages, had become the captain of a merchantman at the age of twenty-four. On retiring from the sea he purchased a glass factory in New Jersey, and founded a manufacturing business which, owing to the admirable output of glass bottles, had prospered with the years, and indeed still prospers. My father, after several unsuccessful business adventures, had, owing to his marriage to my mother, been given a partnership in this firm.

My father was a man of fine presence, and of a sanguine, enthusiastic temperament, too impulsive to manage his own affairs by himself; however, being restrained by the caution of his cautious partners, his gifts of imagination were made to contribute to the firm's prosperity. He was, above all, a magnificent salesman; and travelling all over the United States, and offering the firm's wares to the chemists of the rapidly expanding Republic, he exercised upon those apothecaries the gifts of persuasion and blandishment, almost of hypnotization, which were destined later, in European and more exalted spheres, to produce some startling results. However, before he undertook these journeys, he had been placed for some years in charge of the glass factories in New Jersey; and it was in a small New Jersey town, with the romantic name of Millville, that I was born in 1865.

My earliest recollections are tinged with the gleam of those great fiery furnaces which I used to gaze at from a distance. To my infant apprehensions the whole alarming picture, with the half-naked glass-blowers moving like devils among the flames, presented a vivid image of what I believed might very likely be my future fate. For partly owing to the more serious religious tone of my mother's family, but still more (for the darker aspects of Christian doctrine were not much dwelt on by good Quakers) to the lava stream of evangelical revivalism into which my parents were swept away, the notion of Hell formed a fiery background to my childish thoughts; I was always expecting, half in terror, half in thrilled anticipation, to hear the blast of the Last Trumpet, to see the earth and heavens collapse and the sinners led off to their abodes of Eternal Torment.

The old doctrines of the corruption of man and his inevitable doom unless he finds salvation in the conviction of sin, the gift of grace, and a sudden catastrophic, miraculous conversion – this evangelical theology, though I was nourished on it in my youth, and tasted its joys and terrors, has now become utterly alien and strange to me. I cannot

39

reconstruct in imagination that melodramatic world of hopes and terrors. I know, of course, that this body of convictions has an important place in religious history, and that, as a scheme of salvation, millions have fervently believed in it.

My parents, dissatisfied with what they considered the spiritual deadness of Quaker doctrine, welcomed the new outburst in America of revivalism, into which they plunged as into a great flood of life-giving water; and their evangelical activities formed for many years the absorbing interest of their lives. They went to revivalist meetings, they preached, they both wrote innumerable tracts, they converted souls, they lived in constant expectation of the Day of Judgement; and this highly coloured world, with the heights of Heaven above them and the abysses of Hell beneath – this, and not their commonplace and commercial surroundings, formed the environment in which they lived with such feverish excitement. We children naturally caught the infection of this excitement, and were encouraged to embark in our tender years upon these spiritual adventures.

FIRST VISIT TO EUROPE

——— ✽ ———

NOT long after the memorable event of my conversion, our family went to Europe. My father's health had been affected by his combined mercantile and evangelical exertions; a period of rest and change was recommended by his doctors, and it was thought that this rest and change could be best procured in England. So in 1872 we embarked, my sisters and I, with our handsome florid father and our beautiful straightforward Quaker mother.

Both our parents were quite without any anticipation of the extra-ordinary experiences which awaited them. It is not my purpose to tell in any detail the story of these experiences. Let it suffice to say that news had already reached England of my father's gifts and successes as an evangelist; my mother's fame had also spread abroad, and when they arrived in London they were received with an interest which soon became enthusiasm, and finally almost a frenzy, in that strange world of evangelicals which was once so important, but which has now almost disappeared. It was a world, as I remember it, of large, opulent, ruddy aristocrats, living in great London mansions or country houses, and much given to immense collations and extempore prayers and the propagation of innumerable children. These personages often drove up to the house my father rented at Stoke Newington in the London suburbs, and my sisters and I would peep out through the windows at their fine carriages and horses, and would sometimes be presented to some large, friendly, red-faced man or woman whom we would be summoned to meet in the drawing-room. Often too, while our parents were rapt away to earnest conferences, we would be deposited in some country house, either with the Barclays at Monkhams in Essex (Mrs Barclay was by birth one of the Gurneys of Earlham, and we thus became acquainted with the world of which we had heard so much from Friend Gurney in Philadelphia), or else at Broadlands in Hamp-shire, the home of our parents' friends, the Cowper Temples.

41

When our parents had first arrived in England, they had been invited to a drawing-room meeting of leading evangelicals, which was summoned to judge whether their doctrine was perfectly sound according to the strictest standards. All was well save on one point, about which there were dreadful whispers. From something my mother had said or written, it had come to be suspected that she was not altogether sound on the doctrine of Eternal Torment.

Hell, it was known, she believed in, but did she hold that its torments were destined to endure for ever? As a matter of fact, she didn't; and although my father and her friends besought her to conceal this heresy, when the crisis came and the question was put plainly to her in that London drawing-room, with that large company gravely waiting for her answer, a sudden impulse came upon her to tell the truth. She knew that her own and perhaps her husband's career as expositors of the Gospel might be ruined by this avowal; she had agreed that it would be wiser to give evasive answers on this point; but she suddenly felt that if she was questioned she must say what she thought, whatever might be the consequences; and if she had been capable of using such a profane expression she would have told herself that she didn't care a damn.

She could not, she avowed to the assembled company, believe that the God she worshipped as a God of love was capable of such awful cruelty; sinners, of course, He punished, but that He had decreed that their torments should be unending was to her a horrible belief. Her auditors were inexpressibly dismayed by this declaration; the myrtle, in Keats's phrase, 'sickened in a thousand wreaths'; the company was on the point of breaking up in confusion when from the depths of that great drawing-room there floated forward, swathed in rich Victorian draperies and laces, a tall and stately lady, who kissed my mother, and said, 'My dear, I don't believe it either.'

This dramatic moment was, perhaps, a turning point in my life, since, if it had not occurred, our family would no doubt have soon returned to America, and the ties and friendships which drew us all back again to England would never have been formed. For this lady who thus intervened and took my mother under her protection was, as it were, the queen of evangelical Christians; and her acceptance, afterwards confirmed by that of her husband, William Cowper

Temple, silenced all opposition and no further objections were suggested.

The Cowper Temples, owing to their great wealth and high position, were by far the most important people in the world in which my parents were, so to speak, on trial. Cowper Temple was in law the son of Earl Cowper, but said to be the son of Lord Palmerston, who had long been Lady Cowper's friend, and who married her when Lord Cowper died. Their son had inherited Lord Palmerston's estates and great house at Broadlands; and the problem of this double paternity, if I may put it so, which was the gossip of the time (gossip which sounded strangely in our Philadelphian ears), had been successfully regulated by the young William Cowper's adding Lord Palmerston's family name of Temple to that of Cowper in a double appellation. After acting as secretary to his unavowed father, he served in several posts in the governments of the time and was raised to the peerage as Lord Mount Temple in 1880. His wife, who had corroborated my mother's view of Hell, is known in the history of art as the friend of the Pre-Raphaelites, and above all as the Egeria of Ruskin, who describes in his *Praeterita* how, when in Rome in 1840, he had first seen the beautiful Miss Tollemache (as she was then), and how, though he never met her, he had haunted the Roman churches on the chance of catching a glimpse of her sweet and statuesque beauty – a kind of beauty which had hitherto been only a dream to him – and how the thought of seeing her, if but in the distance, became, he tells us, the hope and solace of his Roman sojourn. It was only fourteen years later that he was introduced to her in London and became her friend.

Her friendship with my mother lasted till her death in extreme old age. She became a beautiful old saint, in whose character my mother could find only one flaw, if flaw it could indeed be called. Lady Mount Temple could never grasp the difference between right and wrong; when no cruelty was involved she could not see why people should not do what they liked. My mother would try to explain moral distinctions to her, and though Lady Mount Temple would say at the moment that she understood them, they soon faded from her mind.

When Oscar Wilde was out on bail between his two trials, she wrote him a friendly letter, inviting him to pay her a visit, by which letter, Oscar Wilde tells us, he was greatly touched. Her family, the Tollemaches, were a wild family, much given to misbehaviour, and when one or another got in disgrace she would invite the offender to her home and would often send for my mother, as one familiar with right and wrong, to come and help the erring one back to the righteous path. I remember my mother telling of one occasion when a Tollemache, married to a foreign prince, had run away from him with a lover, and then had been placed under Lady Mount Temple's roof to be made to realize the impropriety of her conduct. My mother was as usual summoned, and arrived in her Quaker garb and with her Bible, to help in this work of moral reformation. The Bible was read, there were prayers and exhortations, and all seemed to be going on in a most satisfactory manner, till one day, entering the old lady's writing room, my mother noticed that she was trying to conceal a piece of paper, and, when questioned, she confessed that she was composing a telegram for the lover of the erring lady to come and join them, since, as she put it, she felt that Matilda was feeling so lonely without him.

But all this happened years after the occasion of which I have been writing, on which occasion we were promptly invited to come to Broadlands, whither we soon proceeded, my mother, my father, my two sisters, and myself. Broadlands became thenceforward almost our home in England, and in its ample halls were gathered innumerable guests, to listen to the glad tidings of salvation which had reached the shores of England from across the Atlantic Ocean.

My mother and father had more than once attended camp meetings in America, where, amid primeval forests or by the shore of some mountain lake, evangelicals had been accustomed to gather for holy jubilations (not always unaccompanied by hysterial outbursts in which the Chosen People would scream and dance and roll upon the earth); and as they often described to their hosts these outpourings of the spirit, it occurred to the good Cowper Temples to inaugurate a series of such meetings in their park upon the banks of the Test in England, and this project was successfully carried out. My father was an acceptable preacher at these meetings; but my sincere simple-minded mother, beautiful in her Quaker dress, with her candid gaze and golden hair, was given the name of 'the Angel of the Churches', and her expositions of the Gospels, delivered in the great beautiful eighteenth-century orangery in the Park at Broadlands, attracted the largest audiences, and made those gatherings famous in the religious world. They were unattended, however, by any of the wilder phenomena of the American camp meetings, with which my mother had no sympathy, and I cannot recall the spectacle of any English aristocrats foaming at the mouth or rolling in holy ecstasy upon those Hampshire lawns.

It is odd to me now to reflect that while these meetings were going on at Broadlands, quite possibly Dante Gabriel Rossetti was also in the house in person (while in spirit such immeasurable miles away), for he often, I believe, stayed at Broadlands, and painted some of his pictures and wrote some of his poems there. But if we saw him (and we may have seen him), he made upon us, and could have made, no impression at all.

The beauty of Broadlands, with its park and shining river and the great house, full of history and portraits, and crowded with eminent people earnestly seeking Salvation for their souls, had a great effect upon my childish imagination; and when I now recall this period of our lives I cannot but regard as a fantastic adventure this sudden transference of a family of plain-living, middle-class Philadelphia Quakers into circumstances and surroundings so different from what they had been accustomed to. As a proud little American boy, I treasured up at Broadlands boasts with which to impress the boys at home. I remember especially the glory of one week, when there was a horse-show in Broadlands park, and a special box was provided for the Cowper Temples and their guests. They were too busy, of course, in their search for Salvation to occupy this box, but I loved to sit there all by myself, in the gaze of the whole assembled county, with my little heart almost bursting, even at that early age, with emotions for which the word 'snobbish' is, I fear, the only appropriate name. But there were humiliations, as well as glories, for an American boy in those great houses – above all the wise exclusion of children from the evening dinners, an exclusion unheard of in our American world. When, on our first visit to the Barclays at Monkhams, I was summoned to supper with the Barclay children in the nursery, I bitterly declined the invitation; said I had no appetite, and sat weeping in hungry pride in my bedroom. In the stately halls of Broadlands there was no such interdict; my elder sister dressed herself up as a young lady and went in to dinner with the rest, but in the crowd of guests I was occasionally overlooked; and I remember one occasion, almost worthy of a page in Proust, when the stately procession swept along to the dining-room, and I was left behind. My little heart was full of bitterness and eyes of tears, when the Duchess of Sutherland, a Duchess famous for her beauty, who had noticed my plight as she passed me, considerately left the dining-room and returned and took me by the hand and arranged a seat for me at her side. I should like to think that this was the same Duchess of Sutherland whom my grandfather, in his anxiety for a sight of foreign life behind the scenes, had seen purchasing a rug so many years before. I am afraid, however, that chronology forbids.

There are few human beings more detestable to me than spoiled American children, who, full of their own importance, demand continual attention, and are the ruin of all rational talk among grown-up people. But my hatred of these noisy little monsters is – or at least it ought to be – tempered by the recollection that I was in my childhood one of them myself, and must have been at Broadlands a nuisance, which my American parents would, of course, have done nothing to abate.

That the five of us, my father, my mother, my two sisters, and myself, should be invited to stay for weeks and even months in these English country houses gives one an enlarged conception of the hospitality of those times. We children shared governesses with the immense populations of their nurseries, and sometimes attended little local schools in their company. The boys of my own age were naturally my companions; they were for the most part Etonians. Anyone seeking for the home of unspotted purity would probably not pause in his search at an English public school; but the behaviour and conversation of these polite Etonians, though they would have interested Proust, could not have been expected to reveal to the holy little Samuel of Philadelphia anything that was not innocent and pure. I remember one of these boys taking me up into a walnut tree in his father's park, and treating me to a display which, though it had no interest for me at the time, yet I felt, as a mark of friendliness from an English to an American boy, was a demonstration of international goodwill.

WALT WHITMAN

———— ❈ ————

IN 1882, returning home for the Easter holidays, I was told important news by my sister Mary, when she too arrived for her holidays from Smith College (for the ban on the college education of girls was now removed). There was a poet, she informed me and the rest of our family, a great American poet and prophet, – though most Americans were not at all aware of his greatness, – now living in poverty and neglect among us in America, living actually not far from our neighbourhood, and it was her purpose, she informed us, to go without delay and offer him a due tribute of praise and admiration. How had she heard of this poet? her perturbed relatives inquired. A lady lecturer, she replied, had come from Boston to Smith College, and had praised his works, which she had herself immediately ordered from Boston, and which had revealed to her a message of tremendous import, and the purpose of her intended visit was to discuss this message. Consternation fell upon us all, and my father at once forbade it. He vaguely knew the name of the poet, which was by no means a name of good repute in Philadelphia; the district in which he lived was a district not visited by people who respected their own position; no daughter of his, he peremptorily declared, should, while she lived under his roof, be allowed to take so unseemly a step.

My father's refusal to permit this indecorum, though impressive as the poor man could make it, had no effect whatsoever upon my sister. She thought of going, she said, on the following Thursday; and my father, being in his heart well aware of the powerlessness of American parents in their dealings with their daughters, and convinced, as he was, that if my sister meant to go on Thursday, on Thursday she would go, wisely, if unheroically, decided that the best thing under the circumstances was for him to accompany her, and thus lend an air of propriety to the visit. I was invited to join the party, and so on Thursday afternoon off we started from our home in Germantown, behind my father's fine pair of horses. We flashed along through Fairmount Park, we drove across Philadelphia, we embarked in the ferry and crossed the Delaware, and dashed up before the little two-story wooden house in Camden to which we had been directed. An elderly woman who answered the doorbell ushered us into a little parlour and shouted upstairs, 'Walt, here's some carriage folk come to see you.' We heard a stirring above us as of a slow and unwieldy person, and soon through the open door we saw two large feet in carpet slippers slowly descending the stairs, and then the bulky form of the old man appeared before us. Walt Whitman greeted us with friendly simplicity; he had no notion who we were, and we had no introduction to him, but the unannounced appearance of these 'carriage folk' from across the river – this portly and opulent-looking gentleman with his tall son and beautiful tall daughter – did not seem to surprise him in the least. My sister informed him that our name was Smith, that she had read his *Leaves of Grass*, and had come to express her immense admiration for that volume, and this explanation was received with great complacency; we were all invited to follow him upstairs to his den, where we sat down on what chairs could be hastily provided, and were soon engaged in lively talk.

My father, who at first held himself aloof in the most disapproving manner, soon, to the surprise of my sister and myself, began to join in this friendly conversation, and we were still more surprised, when we got up to take our departure, to hear our impulsive parent invite the object of his grave disapprobation to drive back with us to Germantown and spend the night. The afternoon was, he urged, a fine one, the drive across the Park would be pleasant, and it would be a pity to bring to a premature end so agreeable a confabulation. 'No, Mr Smith, I think I won't come,' the poet answered; but when he had hobbled to the window and seen, waiting in the street outside, my father's equipage, he said that he thought he might as well come after all, and, hastily putting a nightshirt and a few other objects in a little bag, he hobbled downstairs and we all drove off together. It was, as my father had said, a pleasant afternoon; we crossed again the ferry, we drove through Philadelphia and through the Park to our home in Germantown, where Walt Whitman remained with us for a month, and whither he would often afterwards return. He became indeed a

48

familiar and friendly inmate of the house, whose genial presence, even when we did not see him, could hardly pass unnoticed, for he had the habit of singing 'Old Jim Crow' when not occupied in conversation, and his loud and cheerful voice could be heard echoing every morning from the bathroom or the water closet. His arrivals were always unannounced; he would appear when he liked, stay as long as he liked; and then one morning we would find at breakfast a pencilled note to say that he had departed early, having had for the present enough of our society.

The reputation which the author of *Leaves of Grass* had acquired by that daring and not decent publication was a dubious one in America at that time; this reputation had reached our Quaker suburb, and our neighbours and relations avoided our house, and forbade their children to visit it, when it was known that Walt Whitman was staying with us. There was, indeed, a grave charge which could have been brought against him, and which would have greatly shocked us all, if we had known (as we fortunately did not) anything about it. There can be no doubt, I fear, that from his boyhood Walt Whitman had associated with Hicksite Quakers, that his father and mother had been followers of this prophet – and that he himself had in his youth heard him preach. Indeed, in his old age he wrote a eulogy of this aged Quaker in which he described the long life of piety and benevolence of the saintly old man, and quoted without the least disapproval his doctrine that true religion consisted, not in sermons and ceremonials, but in spirituality, purity, and the love of God and man. This eulogy of Elias Hicks was written perhaps by the naughty old poet while he was staying under our roof. But, as I say, one's sense of wrong grows weaker with the years, and the other day I read Walt Whitman's account of Elias Hicks with no overwhelming moral condemnation. Indeed it was difficult at any time for anyone to retain a prejudice against Walt Whitman for long. His manners were grand and primeval, like those of the old patriarchs and bards in a picture of Blake's; he treated all people with the same politeness, and only on one occasion did we notice in him any sense of times and occasions and the demands of social etiquette. He had arrived on a visit in a knitted vest, and, when told that a number of people were coming that evening to dinner, the thought occurred to him that probably he ought to put on a coat for the occasion, and after some meditation he appeared at dinner-time a consummate man of the world in his overcoat, thus sacrificing his comfort, for the night was hot, to the demands of the occasion.

Almost every afternoon my father would take Walt Whitman driving in the Park; it was an unfailing interest to them to drive as close as they could behind buggies in which pairs of lovers were seated, and observe the degree of slope towards each other, or 'buggy-angle', as they called it, of these couples; and if ever they saw this angle of approximation narrowed to an embrace, my father and Walt Whitman, who had ever honoured that joy-giving power of nature symbolized under the name of Venus, would return home with happy hearts.

My acquaintanceship with this great and famous poet, – for Walt Whitman had already become famous in England, and his glory had flashed back across the Atlantic to Boston, and thence, as I have described, to where we sat in Germantown in darkness, – the familiar presence of this poet in our house must have had an influence upon me which was more powerful than anything that I was aware of at the time. He was, as John Burroughs has well described him, 'large and picturesque of figure, slow of movement, tolerant, receptive, democratic and full of charity and goodwill towards all. His life was a poet's life from first to last – free, unworldly, unhurried, unconventional, unselfish, and was contentedly and joyously lived.' He was already old and half-paralysed when we made his acquaintance, but of the disabilities of age he never spoke, although their shadows are not absent from his poems of this period. In one of these, for instance, 'Queries to My Seventieth Year', which was written at about the time we came to know him, he thus addresses the oncoming year:

Approaching, nearing curious,
Thou dim, uncertain spectre – bringest thou life or death?
Strength, weakness, blindness, more paralysis and heavier?
Or placid skies and sun? Wilt stir the waters yet?
Or haply cut me short for good? Or leave me here as now,
Dull, parrot-like and old, with crack'd voice harping, screeching?

It was, however, the calm serenity of age, its placid skies and sun, which diffused about him that atmosphere of peace and leisure which made his companionship so genial, and our endless conversations with him so great a pleasure. He was fond of talking with young people, and would listen with the utmost good nature to our crude notions; and when he was not with us, my sisters and I would often visit him in Camden, where on summer days we would find him seated at his window, fanning himself with a large palm-leaf fan, and gazing out on the lazy sunshine that filled his little street. Not infrequently during our visits he would recognize some working-man of his acquaintance as he passed, and call out, 'Come up, Bill, and meet some friends of mine,' and the working-man would come in, or the passing postman, or the driver of an express wagon, and we would all share an improvised meal together.

The floor of the room upstairs in which he lived was covered to the depth of a foot or so with a sea of papers, and now and then he would stir this pool with his stick and fish up a letter from an English admirer – Tennyson, perhaps, or Symonds, or Edward Dowden – or some newspaper article about 'the Good Grey Poet'. Walt Whitman, who had been himself so long a newspaper writer, was curiously fond of newspaper publicity; his floor was strewn with press cuttings in which his name was mentioned, and he would even, I believe, now and then, write anonymous articles about himself for insertion in the local papers. Otherwise he was quite free from literary vanity, and never spoke of his writings unless we questioned him. Then, however, he would answer with great simplicity and frankness.

My sister Mary (whom he called his 'bright, particular star') recalls how once, when she was on the Camden ferry, she saw an Englishman also on the boat. He must, she rightly concluded, be on a pilgrimage like herself to visit Walt Whitman, for how otherwise account for the presence of that Englishman? She, therefore, accosted the correct and dapper figure, who confessed, with some surprise, that this was in fact his purpose. My sister offered to show him the way to Walt Whitman's house, and they proceeded thither, to find, however, that the door was locked and they could get no answer to their knockings. 'I'm sure he's upstairs,' my sister said; 'he always is, so the best thing is for me to boost you up to the window, which you can open, and then come down and let me in.' Edmund Gosse (for the Englishman was Edmund

Gosse) seemed considerably surprised, my sister says, by the uncon-
ventionality of this proposal, but as he had come a long way to visit
Walt Whitman, and did not wish to be baffled in his object, he finally
allowed my sister to boost him up; and then he descended to open the
front door to her, and they found Walt Whitman as usual in his study,
and their visit was a satisfactory one in every way. It is only fair,
however, to add that when, thirty or forty years after, I arranged for
Mrs Berenson and Sir Edmund Gosse to meet at luncheon, the latter,
though admitting that he had met my sister at Walt Whitman's, angrily
denied the boosting and his informal entrance. Knowing both Gosse
and my sister to be endowed with more picturesque than accurate
memories, I have never been able to decide which of them was telling
the truth.

I remember once speaking to Walt Whitman about his poem, 'With
husky-haughty lips O sea!' which had just been published, and he told
me, sitting one summer evening on our porch in Germantown, of the
way he had come to write it; how always, from the days of his boyhood
on the Long Island coasts, he had tried and tried again to seize the
meaning which the voice of the ocean was always whispering in his
ears; how often by day, and more often by night, he had sat or lain
amid the sandhills on its margin, listening in a kind of torment of
attention to that great voice – some voice – in what words could he
best describe it?

– some voice, in huge monotonous rage, of freedom-lover pent,
Some vast heart, like a planet's, chain'd and chafing in those
breakers.

This notion of receptivity to experience, and of a complete surrender
to it, combined with a patient effort to grasp its deepest meaning and
to embody that meaning in significant words – this account of the old
man's poetic method, as he told it one summer evening, was deeply
impressive to his boyish listener, although that listener had then no
thought of attempting to coin his own experience into enduring metal.
To melt material sand into saleable glass bottles – this, he believed,
was to be his destiny; and the idea that all such massy unmetaphorical
gold might be gladly bartered – as Walt Whitman would gladly have

bartered it – for the ability to embody in words some one of Nature's aspects – the sea's voice, for instance, or the breath of its salt fragrance, or even, as he himself had said, 'the undulation of one wave', – the idea of so mad a preference would have seemed to his youthful listener at that date fantastic indeed.

Thus I listened to the impressive talk of the old poet, and though I had no notion of following his example, the effect upon me of his poems, as I read and reread that strange volume, *Leaves of Grass* – how can I adequately describe it? There are books which come to us like revelations, which, as Emerson says, 'take rank in our lives with parents and lovers and passionate experiences', and to come on such a book to which one can yield oneself in absolute surrender – there is no intellectual enjoyment, I believe, no joy of the mind greater in youth than this. Books of this kind should be contemporary books, written by the living for the living; and should present us with a picture of life as we ourselves know it and feel it. And they should above all reveal us to ourselves, should hold up a looking-glass before our eyes in which we see our own faces. Much that was suppressed in the young people of my generation found a frank avowal in *Leaves of Grass*; feelings and affections for each other, which we had been ashamed of, thoughts which we had hidden as unutterable, we found printed in its pages, discovering that they were not, as we had believed, the thoughts and feelings of young, guilty, half-crazy goblins, but portions of the Kingdom of Truth and the same experience of mankind. It was above all Walt Whitman's rejoicing in his flesh and blood, – 'there is so much of me', he sang, 'and all so luscious,' – his delight in his own body and the bodies of his friends, which seemed a revelation and gave *Leaves of Grass* so strong a hold upon a generation born of puritans who had ignored, or treated as shameful, those habitations of the spirit. Then, too, Walt Whitman's affection for his fellow human beings, – for he was one of those rare spirits who really love the human race, – his feeling that all men and women, of whatever race or class and in whatever state of degradation, were all of them not worthless and of no account, but lovable and mysterious and divine – this seemed to fill for us the many-peopled world with innumerable creatures, all dear and infinitely precious. These were the streams of life which flowed from that fountain; and catching also from its pages the fervour of his exultant pride in Democracy, in America and the age we lived in, and moved also by the splendid passages here and there of great poetry, it is no wonder that we came to regard as a sacred book the vast printed chaos of *Leaves of Grass*. It gave us ears, it gave us eyes, it revealed to us the miracle of our own existence, and for me, at least, with my meagre ideals of borrowed culture, it seemed to open a great shining window in my narrow house of life.

HARVARD

———— ✳ ————

MY father had given me a generous allowance. I had already a
few acquaintances who belonged to what was considered
a good set among the undergraduates, and was elected a
member of several of those societies and fraternities which play, or
played, so important a part in Harvard life. I have now forgotten the
names of these foolish associations, but my pleasure at my election to
them I can still recall. It was in the essence a snobbish pleasure; why
should I boggle at the word? Indeed the atmosphere of Harvard was at
that time – whether it has changed since then, I do not know – richly
coloured by the sense of social differences. The prestige possessed by
members of the most exclusive clubs, the delight of being seen in their
company, and the hope of being admitted into their select circles –
these were the animating motives of life at Harvard as I knew it; and
the democratic principles I had learned from Walt Whitman were of
little avail against this atmosphere of social aspiration. That there was
an intellectual set at Harvard of much greater interest than the foolish
world in which I was, after all, little more than an outsider; that there
were other young men of intelligence and high promise among my
contemporaries, I had not the slightest notion. I was indeed hardly
worthy at that time of the notice of intellectuals like Santayana and
Berenson, who were at Harvard with me, though I did not know them,
and with whom I became acquainted only in after years.

I actually sat beside my present brother-in-law, Berenson, at a
course of William James's lectures, but no communication passed
between us, and it was not till long afterwards, when he had married
my elder sister, that we began that series of confabulations to which I
owe so much. For my parents' sake William James did, however,
befriend their callow offspring, and I was often invited to his hospitable house. I need not try to describe the charm of the most charming
man I ever met; Ralph Perry has performed that task in his admirable

biography, but I may add perhaps a touch to his account of that free and spontaneous spirit by repeating an anecdote he related to me one night, telling me that I might repeat it anywhere but in Cambridge.

He had gone, he told me, by tram that afternoon to Boston; and as he sat and meditated in the Cambridge horse-car two strains of thought had occupied his mind. One of these was the notion, which Mrs James had recently derived from the perusal of Kipling's writings, that our civil order, that all the graces and amenities of our social life, had for their ultimate sanction nothing but force, however much we might disguise it – the naked fist, in fact, the blow of the sword, the crack of the pistol, or the smoke and roar of guns. Superimposed upon this meditation began to recur, with greater and greater persistence, the memory of certain remarks of his brother Henry, who, on a recent visit to America had indignantly protested against the outrageous pertness of the American child and the meek pusillanimity with which the older generation suffered the behaviour of their children without protest.

It was not long, William James said, before he became aware of what had aroused this second line of thought; it was the droning sound which filled the horse-car – the voice, in fact, of an American child, who was squeaking over and over again an endless, shrill, monotonous singsong. Growing more and more irritated by this squeaking, William James resolved that he at least would not suffer it without protest; so, addressing the mother of the vocal infant, he said politely, 'I think, madam, you can hardly be aware that your child's song is a cause of annoyance to the rest of us in this car.' The lady thus addressed paid no attention; but a gallant American, who had heard it, turned on him and said with great indignation, 'How dare you, sir, address a lady in this ungentlemanly fashion!' At this insult William James, recalling the doctrine of naked force which his wife had impressed upon him, replied with manly promptness, 'Sir, if you repeat that remark, I shall slap your face.' The remark, to his consternation, was repeated, and the professor was compelled to make good his word. The slap was conscientiously administered; the occupants of the horse-car arose in indignation, pressing their cards upon the victim of the assault, and protesting their willingness to be witnesses at any legal proceedings which might ensue. Then they all sat down; and as the car clattered along through the dust towards Boston, with the child still shrilly singing, the grave burden of the public disapproval which William James had encountered became almost more, he said, than he could bear.

He looked from hostile face to hostile face, longing for some sign of sympathy and comprehension, and fixed at last all his hopes on a lady who had taken no part in the uproar, and whose appearance suggested foreign travel perhaps, or at any rate a wider point of view. He felt that she at least understood the motive of his action; and so great was his longing for sympathy that when at last the car reached Boston and they all got out he committed the error of trying to make sure of her approbation. 'You, madam,' he said, addressing her, 'you, I feel sure, will understand . . .' Thereupon the lady drew back from him and exclaimed, 'You brute!'

I may add here another anecdote of William James, for when I name that enchanting person it is difficult to dismiss him with no further mention. Some years later, when our family was at last established abroad, he came to stay with us in Sussex, and declared his desire to spend a summer in England and experience the joys of English country life. My father thereupon obtained a list of country houses to be let in the neighbourhood, and orders to view them, and drove William James to see one after the other. This inspection he carried on with the utmost care, examining each house from attic to cellar, allotting the various rooms to be occupied by the various members of his family. When this process was over, and the gardens and even the stables had been examined, and he returned to our house to dinner, he genially remarked, 'I can't tell you how grateful I am for all the trouble you have taken; I have had my summer in England, and now we go abroad.'

While we were at Harvard, Edmund Gosse came to Boston to deliver the Lowell Lectures; my sister and many of the Harvard intellectuals went religiously to listen to the utterance of this English writer, whose name was familiar to us all. Of these lectures I have forgotten everything except one pregnant sentence, in which the name of Botticelli first echoed in our ears. 'Botticelli', the lecturer said, in that cultivated 'English accent' which was music to us, 'Botticelli', – and with what unction he slowly reiterated those syllables! – 'Botticelli, that name which is an open sesame to the most select, the most distinguished, the most exclusive circles of European culture.' The effect of these words upon us was magical. What longings it aroused in us, what delicious provincial aspirations for a world fairer than the world we lived in – for exquisite, remote, European things! It was the song the Syrens sang, it was the voice of the Muses that Thamyris heard among the Theban mountains, it was almost the voice that summoned Saint Paul to a higher life as he journeyed to Damascus. Would Fate, we deliciously wondered, ever vouchsafe to us to enunciate those syllables of sweet magic and thus win admission to those far-away bright circles of European culture, circles as heavenly in our provincial eyes as those circling rings of angels seen in great Italian pictures? Among that audience, although my sister and I did not know him at the time, was the future art critic, Bernard Berenson, who, he has told us since, went at once and bought himself a reproduction of Botticelli's 'Primavera'.

Life is an ironic thing, and when years afterwards I recalled to Sir Edmund Gosse the words which he had pronounced long ago in Boston, he told me that his principal association with the name of Botticelli at that time was connected with the family cat, Beneder, which was then by its mewings causing considerable annoyance in his household. There had been a joke in *Punch* about an æsthete who, when shown a picture attributed to Botticelli, had denied its authenticity on the ground that he was always dumb in the presence of the work of that master. So the Gosses had purchased a photograph of an unquestioned picture by Botticelli, and pinned it up by the basket of Beneder, in the hope, which proved a vain one, of silencing its voice.

I have spoken of the effect upon me of Walt Whitman's poems; I fell at Harvard (for my time there was not utterly wasted) under the influence of another living writer, Matthew Arnold. When I now think of Matthew Arnold, it makes me rather sad. The exquisite poet who so soon abandoned poetry; the supreme critic whose best criticism is so scanty; the great writer who wasted the energy of his best years in dull official routine; the advocate of Hellenism and sweet reasonableness who soon gave himself up to angry recrimination, and who, whether owing to exasperation with his contemporaries or to some arrogant streak in his own nature, more and more abandoned that serene aloofness from contemporary conflicts which had been his ideal, and adopted a pose of aggressive, self-satisfied contempt, and a harsh browbeating style full of derisive catchwords.

When I read again the best writings of Matthew Arnold I find in them the expression of the most truly enlightened spirit among the great Victorians, the most humane, the most European and least provincial of all English authors, whose outlook is still our outlook, who still speaks to us with contemporary accents. But fifty years ago it was that more controversial Matthew Arnold who aroused my young enthusiasm. His aggressive warfare with the Philistines delighted me; I rejoiced in his ridicule of the evangelical religion and dissent in which I had been nourished, and what delighted me most of all was his attribution of an arrogant superiority, an exclusive kind of distinction to that culture, that sweetness and light, which now for the flimsiest reasons I believed that I had attained. But it was not only the attainment of culture for oneself, but the diffusion of it, which Matthew Arnold preached, and this part of his doctrine was most of all an inspiration to me.

I belonged by family traditions to the philanthropic world; from the American atmosphere and from the conversations and the writings of Walt Whitman I had absorbed democratic principles which floated vaguely – as such principles can easily float without conflict – side by side with my more exclusive proclivities, and above all with an ideal of cultural uplift, as it would now be called. I found that I could gild with a finer gold than that of dollars my future commercial prospects. I imagined myself as returning when I entered the family business, to my birthplace amid its furnaces in New Jersey, to diffuse among those raw and illiberal workmen a love of beauty, a passion for things of the mind and a desire to learn the best that is known and thought in the world. I saw myself a picturesque, a somewhat pathetic figure (for the children of light are lonely in this world and are almost always persecuted by it), awakening in these unenlightened employees of my family their more delicate and spiritual perceptions, and by a most happy combination of circumstances drawing all the while a large income from my activities among them.

Thus Matthew Arnold's oft-repeated watchwords of 'sweetness and light', and 'warfare against the Philistines' were words of enchantment in my ears; and another doctrine of his, that of 'many-sided culture', served usefully also to justify and ennoble the extremely many-sided, not to say miscellaneous studies – if they may be called studies – which engaged a small part of my attention during my sojourn at Harvard.

Following the example and enjoying the companionship of my gay and unstudious companions, I had fallen in with the strange custom which then prevailed at that university (things are changed now for the better, I believe) of attending miscellaneous and perfectly unrelated lecture-courses – courses recommended more for what was called their 'softness' than for any other reason; going to lectures, for instance, at the same time on Dante and Meteorology, on Homer and on the practice of philanthropy, and other unconnected subjects. If this was a strange method of acquiring the many-sided culture Matthew Arnold recommended, its strangeness never occurred to me, nor was it ever suggested by any of my instructors.

I perceive that I got almost nothing of intellectual value from Harvard University. It was my fault, no doubt; if I had been a real student, I should have found genuine instruction. But, for all my assumption of superiority, the crudeness of my mind at the age of twenty wakens amazement in me. Though I read the works of Matthew Arnold, I gave equal or perhaps more serious attention to the literature of Theosophy, and was inclined to believe that the key to the problem of existence was to be found, if I could only grasp it, in a little book of Rosicrucian doctrine over which I used to pore for hours. My sister, with her superior philosophic light, scorned my Rosicrucian speculations, but she herself visited at this time, with the intention of studying her doctrine, the famous female prophet, Mrs Mary Baker Eddy; nor was she much better able than I to discriminate between all the various names – Botticelli and Benjamin Jowett and Mrs Eddy and Matthew Arnold and Gladstone and William James and the Rosy Cross – which sounded in our ears.

I detect in myself a tendency to sentimentalize over these early years of my existence. It is not that I wish to recall my youth. It is rather that I feel a kind of impatient pity for that half-baked young fool of an American boy about whom I have been writing. No, I have no regrets for youth. Gladly would I go on living at my present age, and with my present interests, for uncounted years. To become young again would seem to me an appalling prospect. Youth is a kind of delirium, which can only be cured, if it is ever cured at all, by years of painful treatment.

The debt of our civilization to the ancient Greeks is of course beyond all calculation, but in one respect we have no cause to thank them. Their adoration of the youthful human form, in contrast to the Eastern idealization of venerable age, has put a kind of blight on human life; our progress, as we grow older, in wisdom and humanity is thought of in terms of the physical decay which accompanies that luminous advance. We feel ashamed, instead of feeling proud, like the Chinese, of our accumulating years; we are always trying in vain to seem younger than we really are; and.in our Western world it is by no means a compliment, as it is in the wise East, to attribute to others a greater age than their appearance might suggest. When I think of that brother and sister fifty years ago at Harvard, – endowed, it may be, with the grace of youth, but full otherwise of ignorance and folly, – I cannot but prize more highly our present state. Our bones are ripening, it is true, for their ultimate repose, but how small a price, after all, is that to pay for the knowledge we have acquired of the world and men, for the splendid panorama of literature and the arts which years of travel and study have unrolled before us, and above all for those adequate conceptions in whose possession, according to Spinoza's wisdom, true felicity consists.

OXFORD

———— ✳ ————

M Y flight from America occurred in 1888. My sister Mary was by that time married and settled in London, and her barrister husband insisted with great emphasis that I should be transferred without delay to what was, in his opinion, the only nursing home of reasonable thought and noble ambition – in fact, to Balliol College. There the spirit of T. H. Green and of Arnold Toynbee was still potent, and there the great Benjamin Jowett still lived and reigned. This had all been happily arranged, and the change from America to England, from a New York counting-house to Oxford, seemed to me a piece of flawless good fortune. But there is a flaw, unluckily, as Emerson pointed out, in everything God has made; and I am inclined to believe now, as I muse in retrospect on these events of fifty years ago, that two slight incidents, though I saw no significance in them at the time, might without superstition be regarded as the first faint foreshadowings of the tiny rift which was destined to flaw a little the felicity of my residence in England.

Both are trivial matters, both absurd in character, the first hardly worth mentioning at all. I had reached London in advance of my luggage; my father and I were to dine the evening of our arrival with Lord and Lady Mount Temple in their great house in Stanhope Gate, and I appeared in those stately halls, at what was my first London dinner party, in dress clothes hired for the evening. My second false step was one the gravity of which Oxford men will appreciate – indeed, I shrink from mentioning it, even at the distance of fifty years. I was to travel to Oxford the next day to interview Benjamin Jowett, and I performed the journey by the London-Midland Railway from Euston Station with a change of trains at Bletchley – an unheard of method of approach, which is nevertheless given in the railway guide as an alternative to the swift and direct journey by the Great Western from Paddington. Since the distances and prices were almost identical, how was I to know the gigantic error of the route I chose?

The great Jowett, who had of course no notion that I came from Euston, received me kindly; the entrance examination to Balliol was, I must think, made easy for me, and I was taken at once into the pleasant household of A. L. Smith, later the Master of Balliol, to prepare for that examination to the University, or 'Smalls', which no personal favour could modify or make easy. The little smattering of Latin and Greek which I acquired in America had faded from my mind; I was forced to begin again with the Greek alphabet. But I was anxious to learn, my tutor had a real genius for teaching, and in about three months' time I acquired that minimum of classical learning which was then necessary for admission to the University, and took up my residence in Balliol. I see myself as being at that time an easy, pleasant, well-meaning, plausible youth, older in years than my English comrades (for I was twenty-three), but in mind and education much cruder than almost any of them, though they were young and crude enough. I was the only or almost the only American in Oxford; for it was long before the great invasion had begun. I was liked, or at any rate I was kindly tolerated.

Jowett, as is well known, was the victim all his life of an absurd social shyness, a shyness he diffused about him like a kind of terror. To this I was, however, immune. I claim no credit for my lack of becoming awe; it was part of my American simplicity, and I can recall with a kind of amazement those dinner parties of his to which he would ask a few undergraduates to meet the distinguished guests who so often stayed with him. There, with their wives, were Cabinet Ministers who could face a howling House of Commons but could not face the Master; famous travellers who had looked on danger with unflinching eyes but who now were paralysed with shyness: all were as frightened of the Master as he was terrified of them, all sat tongue-tied as in a nightmare. It was very odd; but what seems to me now the oddest feature of these occasions is the fact that I was there, an undergraduate, a clerk released not many months before from a New York office, monopolizing the conversation. Among all those eminent people the only words which were heard were often spoken in my transatlantic accent. But being young and inexperienced in the world, I regarded situations as simple which were full in fact of complications; hating to see people uncomfortable and embarrassed, I wanted to help them feel at ease. My host must have been grateful to me, as he kept asking me to his parties. I remember once how, when I stood looking across the chasm which yawned in his drawing-room between his London guests and the undergraduates invited in after dinner, I saw some London acquaintances of mine and stepped across the gulf to greet them, and how the Master gave me a little pat on the back and murmured, 'That's a brave young gentleman.'

But the state of society I am now describing must, I think, have vanished long ago. Eminent Englishmen now meet (except, perhaps, in royal circles) without undue embarrassment or shyness; since the death of Lord Kitchener I doubt if there is anyone who can make them shake in their shoes; and certainly the American accent is familiar, if not too familiar, to them all.

Who were the eminent personages I met at the Master's dinner parties? That they were large and shy is almost all I remember about them; I was too ignorant of contemporary life in England to attach much meaning to their names. They have faded from my memory with the exception of Lord Dufferin, of whom Harold Nicolson has just written a delightful portrait. I have a reason, somewhat beneath the dignity of history, to remember this ex-Viceroy of India, this ex-Governor-General of Canada, who was at the time, I believe, British Ambassador in France. On arriving at the Master's I was presented to him and his wife, who happened to make a gesture which struck me as rather odd. I paid, however, but little attention to it, as the Marquis immediately drew me apart and began talking to me in that manner full of fascination for which he was justly famous. I was naturally flattered by the way I had been singled out and drawn aside from the company upon which he turned his back, until I noticed that while he talked he was busy adjusting his costume. The odd gesture of the Marchioness had plainly been an agreed signal of a misplaced ambassadorial button which it was her high concern to put right.

Jowett not only asked me to his dinner parties, but invited me also to stay with him in his Malvern cottage. I only knew him, of course, in his old age; his work was over, he was enjoying a deserved repose after the efforts and battles of his earlier career, and the worldly disillusioned old man was by no means an inspiration to earnest youth. He had known so many idealists; he had been an idealist himself, and the gospel he preached had changed by now into a gospel of wet blanket. Aspirations expressed in his hearing met with no encouragement. 'People are seldom better employed than in earning their own living' was a favourite aphorism of his. I remember the experience of a Balliol contemporary of mine whose ambition it was to devote himself to the pursuit of Truth. His mother, perplexed by this odd notion of her offspring, came to Oxford and took her son with her to consult the Master on the project. The youth stammered out with the enthusiasm of youth this ideal of a dedicated life, like Spinoza's. Jowett listened, looking like an old pink and white parrot. There was then a pause, in which mother and son waited anxiously for his verdict, which was: 'You can get it up to £900 a year, perhaps, but no more than that.'

Taking essays to read to Jowett, as in groups of two or three we used to take them, was a terrifying but also a most amusing experience. He would listen with his head cocked on one side, ready to peck at any fine sentiments or fine writing; and it was his favourite device to pretend that he had not heard the offending passage. 'Read that again,' he would request, in his squeaky voice; and then would come his comment. I remember once, when Macaulay was the subject of the week's essay, hearing a Scottish scholar of the college begin with a strong Scottish accent, 'It is strange that anyone should have read so much and thought so little. It is strange that anyone should have done so much and lived so little.' I thought this beginning full of promise, but Jowett, after insisting on its being read twice again, squeaked, 'That sentence has no meaning; I must ask you to write your essay again from the very beginning.' But once, rumour said, the Master had been completely nonplussed; an undergraduate had begun his essay with the sentence, 'All social reformers from Socrates and Jesus Christ to Bradlaugh and Annie Besant' (best known at that time as advocates of atheism and birth-control). 'Read that again,' snapped Jowett; it was read again, it was read three times, and then – the Master said nothing.

I grew really fond of Jowett, though he fell far short of my priggish approbation. Any earnest student who made the slightest slip was severely punished by him, while the drunken escapade of some rowdy aristocrat would meet with the mildest of reproofs. It was perhaps part of this mellow naughtiness of his that he seemed inclined to encourage my avowed intention of devoting myself to the fine art of writing. It was an aspiration he had never before encountered; he had, perhaps – who knows? – a secret sympathy with it, for he was a writer of admirable prose himself. Anyhow, he knew that such an ideal was absolutely not catching, and I dare say he was aware that the Balliol Dons who were entrusted with my education would be annoyed by any such notion; and Jowett did not in the least mind annoying the Dons of Balliol.

But these Dons of Balliol, these 'Greats' tutors who supervised my work for the Schools, though they were infinitely courteous and painstaking, had much more serious reasons for disliking me (as I am sure they did dislike me) than any fantastic desire of mine to be a writer. My mind, though they may have dimly hoped at first that it could be coached to win First-Class honours for the college, must have seemed to them sadly lacking, as indeed it was, in discipline and training. I think that by a kind of instinct they realized that I had come to Oxford from Euston, and that no subsequent drilling could repair the error of this Midland journey.

Sir Walter Raleigh describes in one of his letters a paper read in his research class at Oxford by a Rhodes Scholar. 'It was empty, magniloquent, abstract, flatulent, pretentious, confused, and sub-human. I could have wept salt tears. But I couldn't do anything else; the young man wanted a clean heart and a new spirit, not a little top-dressing.' All these adjectives would, I am sure, apply to the essays I used to read to these long-suffering tutors. They must have felt acutely my need of the clean heart and a new spirit; and so conscientiously did they attempt to supply me with them that now for the very first time in my life I was, as we say, 'up against it' – this was my first contact with real education, with the standards of real scholarship and thought.

The Oxford School of *Literae Humaniores* – or 'Greats', as it is called – seems to my mature judgement the best scheme of education that I have ever heard of. It is based upon an accurate knowledge of Greek and Latin texts, especially the texts of Plato and Aristotle and Thucydides and Tacitus, and the subjects studied in it are the eternal problems of thought, of conduct, and of social organization. These are discussed, not by means of contemporary catchwords, but by translating them back into another world and another language. Nor could anything be more profitable from the pupil's point of view than the way in which this scheme of education was carried out. The student would prepare a paper on some special subject and go with it, generally alone, and read it to his tutor, who would then discuss it and criticize it at length; or a group of two or three would meet in the tutor's room for a kind of Socratic discussion of some special point. These discussions were carried on much in the spirit of the Socratic dialogues; and the Socratic irony and assumed ignorance of the instructors, their deferential questions, as if the pupil were the teacher and they the learners, was a method which I found it hard at first to understand.

I remember, for instance, in reading a paper to Nettleship, I mentioned the distinction between form and matter. 'Excuse me for interrupting you,' Nettleship said, 'but this distinction you make, though it is no doubt most important, is one that I find a little difficult to grasp. If it is not troubling you too much, it would be a real kindness if you would try to explain it to me.'

'Oh, it's quite simple,' I answered patronizingly. 'There's the idea, say, in a poem, and there's the way in which it is expressed.'

Nettleship still seemed puzzled. 'Could you give me an instance?' he pleaded.

'Oh, nothing easier,' I answered. 'Take the lines, for instance, when Lovelace says,

> I could not love thee, dear, so much,
> Loved I not honour more.

Now he might have said, "I couldn't be nearly so fond of you, my dear, if I didn't care still more for my reputation." The form, you see, is very different in both these sentences, but the subject of them – what they mean – is exactly the same.'

Nettleship seemed greatly discouraged. 'I'm afraid,' he said, 'I can't see that the meaning of the two sentences is the same. I'm afraid I'm very stupid, but to me they seem to say quite different things.'

He was, I thought, curiously stupid; but in my patient attempt to make my meaning clearer to him a dim suspicion began to waken in me that perhaps it was not Nettleship but I myself who was playing the part of the fool in this dialogue.

The Oxford School of Greats, and the Oxford tutorial system, which had been perfected by Jowett and was seen at its very best in Balliol College, were exactly what I needed to knock out of me my pretentious superficiality; and if I have to any degree attained a 'clean heart and new spirit', I owe it to these years of careful tuition and personal guidance at Balliol. Yet I cannot but feel that this system of personal tuition involved an intolerable waste of fine material, and that it was a fantastic, almost a wicked, thing that hours and hours of the time of men like Nettleship and Abbott and the other Greats tutors should have been devoted to the culture of an intellect so raw and crude as mine.

Nor can I believe that this patient, persistent instruction and spoon-feeding of individuals is the proper function of University teachers, or that, to the best minds already well grounded at school, such additional schoolmastering can be really beneficial. Universities should, it seems to me, be organized, not for the purpose of educating the second-rate and stupid, for transforming at infinite expense of labour the ears of sows into some poor semblance of silk purses, but for the enlightenment and development of the keenest intelligences, for the encouragement by example of original research. Daring and original minds are cramped and injured by being always led in strings and fed on pap which has been carefully prepared for them. They should be allowed to make their profitable mistakes; and, above all, their spirits should be kindled by contact with original scholars and masters of first-hand learning.

To any such ideal the hard-worked college tutor, who had generally begun tutoring the moment he ceased to be a pupil, could have, of course, no chance of attaining. Naturally he tended to depreciate those who attempted to achieve this ideal, and he had not far to look for them. There existed at Oxford, in a kind of shadowy world, a whole body of University professors, men of original learning and research, who were generally appointed from outside, and who lectured on the same subjects as the College tutors. But of all this I had not the slightest notion. My only intimation of it was when I was calling one day on the Regius Professor of Modern History (whom I had met travelling in Sicily) and heard him tell his parlourmaid to run over to his lecture-room across St Giles and see if there were any auditors assembled. In this case, the Professor told me, he would be compelled to attend himself. The maid soon brought back the accustomed news that the lecture room was completely empty, and so we were enabled to have our tea in peace.

My host's predecessor, the great historian Stubbs, had undergone much the same neglect when he came to lecture in Oxford. The trouble was that professors would lecture on the things that interested them, rather than provide information which might prove useful in those examinations in which the colleges competed fiercely with each other, and no college more fiercely than my own. Indeed, it might have easily happened in Oxford at this period (I don't know how it would be now) that the greatest authority in the world might give a lecture on his special subject, and not one of those tutors who taught that subject, or those undergraduates who were engaged in its study, would find it worth his while to attend the lecture. Certainly any desire to do so would have been seriously frowned upon in Balliol, as being likely to interfere with that triumph of Balliol over other colleges which was held before our eyes as the highest and noblest of university aims.

Balliol College, drunk with its triumph in the university examinations, had made success of this kind its glory and ideal, and the immense importance of gaining a First and thus helping to defeat and disconcert and keep down all rival colleges was continually impressed upon us. I remember receiving a dim impression of this passion when I read an essay on some special point in Roman history to my tutor. I had taken an unusual interest in this subject, which I had chosen for myself, and I had read and thought with special thoroughness about it. I was proud of my essay, and my tutor gave it unusual praise, in which praise I was conscious of the mingling of a curious malease. 'Yes,' he said, 'this is an excellent piece of work, the best work of yours I have seen; if all your work were of this quality you might get a First, and do honour to your college. But I'm afraid that, after all, your time has been wasted. That question was asked by the examiners last year.'

This ideal of winning Firsts in examinations for the glory of Balliol was so impressed upon me, that though I have little college patriotism remaining, and an Oxford First has lost all its glory in my eyes, I still study in *The Times* the examination lists and count up the Firsts achieved by the various colleges, and rejoice when, as almost always happens, I find that Balliol still maintains its old pre-eminence.

All the same, this spirit of competition between one college and another seems to me now more schoolboyish and absurd than most forms of patriotic sentiment, and I find it difficult to understand how serious and noble men like the Balliol Dons could have been inspired by such childish ambitions, and done all they could – and they could do much – to inspire others with them. Of course the rational, judicious hatred I entertain for our rival university, Cambridge, being founded on reason and free from prejudice of any kind, is quite another matter, and should not be so much as mentioned here.

The other ideal strongly impressed upon Balliol undergraduates was the duty of getting on in the world; and indeed triumph in examinations was above all praised as the first step on the path to more important triumphs. It has been said of Jowett that he united with high moral and religious seriousness the plain determination that his pupils should not fail of mundane distinction; and, naughty as he may have become in other ways, at worldly success he never mocked. There was much glorification on college occasions of the Balliol men who had achieved high honours and positions. College gaudies were gaudy indeed with the litany of glorious names recited on these occasions – names of viceroys, archbishops, Cabinet ministers, even Prime Ministers who were sons of Balliol, and who not infrequently would return as grateful sons to their *alma mater* and shed their lustre upon the college whence they had first winged their flights. To tell the truth, I came in the end to find these entertainments rather cloying to my taste; and though the roll call of Balliol names has grown with the years even more illustrious, I am inspired with no desire to listen to it. I am glad that members of my college have performed noble services in the world, and have been nobly rewarded by a grateful nation; but loud proclamations of these achievements and reiterated college boastings I find, to tell the truth, rather boring. I should more joyfully attend a gaudy for the black sheep of the college, the scapegraces and ne'er-do-wells; and if men of literary distinction like Matthew Arnold or

Swinburne, or others famous for scholarly or literary research, had been praised on these occasions (which never happened), I should have listened with greater interest.

The word 'research' as a university ideal had, indeed, been ominously spoken in Oxford by that extremely cantankerous person, Mark Pattison, some years ago; but the notion of this ideal, threatening as it did to discredit the whole tutorial and examinational system which was making Oxford into the highest of high schools for boys, was received there with anger and contempt. In Balliol, the birthplace and most illustrious home of this great system, it was regarded with especial scorn. If the prize fellowships and the fellowships at All Souls were to be no longer regarded as the legitimate reward of those who had won First Classes in the Schools; if the means they provided were not to be spent in helping ambitious young men on the first rungs of the ladder of worldly success, but used, as Mark Pattison's ill-mannered supporters suggested, in the maintenance of researchers, ambitious of the fame of scholars, would not the whole tutorial system be deprived of one of its important features, and the university endowments be seriously abused? This ideal of endowment for research was particularly shocking to Benjamin Jowett, the great inventor of the tutorial system which it threatened. I remember once, when staying with him at Malvern, inadvertently pronouncing the ill-omened word. 'Research!' the Master exclaimed. 'Research!' he said. 'A mere excuse for idleness; it has never achieved, and will never achieve any results of the slighest value.' At this sweeping statement I protested, whereupon I was peremptorily told, if I knew of any such results of value, to name them without delay. My ideas on the subject were by no means profound, and anyhow it is difficult to give definite instances of a general proposition at a moment's notice. The only thing that came into my head was the recent discovery, of which I had read somewhere, that on striking a patient's kneecap sharply he would give an involuntary kick, and that by the vigour or lack of vigour of this 'knee jerk', as it is called, a judgement could be formed of his general state of health.

'I don't believe a word of it,' Jowett replied. 'Just give my knee a tap.'

I was extremely reluctant to perform this irreverent act upon his person, but the Master angrily insisted, and the undergraduate could do nothing but obey. The little leg reacted with a vigour which almost alarmed me, and must, I think, have considerably disconcerted that elderly and eminent opponent of research.

I fear that I have succumbed to my love of irony in writing of the tutorial system and Balliol and the Balliol Dons. In all sincerity, however, I feel that I cannot be too grateful to Nettleship, to Strachan Davidson, to Forbes and Abbott, for the unstinted trouble they took to give me the new heart I needed. For all the purposes they cared for I was almost certainly useless: I could not be expected to add to the glory of Balliol either in the Schools or in the world of great affairs; and yet hour after hour they tutored me and listened, I will not say unweariedly, but at any rate without any manifestation of weariness, to my essays. Though I feel sure they did not like me, no sign of this ever appeared in the beautiful courtesy with which I was always treated by them.

Balliol gave me much, gave me some elements of real education, some tincture of the classics; from the spirit of high endeavour fostered in the college I was stimulated to feel that life was an opportunity for achievement, that there were laurels to be gathered and garlands to be run for. But the civic garlands which were prized in Balliol were not really objects of my ambition: I still wished to cultivate the art of letters, and no such notion was encouraged in that college. Indeed, save for a mild appreciation of music, there was at that time no interest in any of the arts in Balliol. The Masters and Fellows had destroyed almost all the antique beauty of the college, building upon its ruins a hideous castle of the Philistines; and it was in this castle, where young Philistines were being trained to go forth and conquer and rule the kingdoms of the world, it was in this castle that I dwelt – high up, in fact, in one of its battlemented towers.

But to me dwelling thus among the children of this world, and toiling with them for that success which leads to worldly advancement; to me, enmeshed as I was in all the social, political, and philanthropic interests of my companions, there floated through the Oxford air, there drifted over the college walls, a voice, whispering, as in the delicate cadences of the Oxford bells, enchantments very unlike anything I heard in the college lecture rooms or chapel. If you would save your soul, the voice seemed to whisper, if you would discover that personal and peculiar sense of life which is your most precious endowment, you must practise and perfect a habit of discrimination; amid all you hear and see you must choose whatever is relevant and significant to you, and only that, rejecting with equal sincerity everything that is not really yours – all the interests you catch from others, all the standards and beliefs and feelings which are imposed on you by the society and the age you live in. Watch above all, the voice admonished me in its grave accents, for those special moments of illumination within, or of visible delight from the world around you, which seem to set free the spirit for a moment. Not to discriminate these visitations of beauty, not thus to respond to them, is, the voice admonished me, on this short day of frost and sunshine, to sleep before evening.

Thus from not far off in space, but across a whole world, as it were, of thought, the voice of Walter Pater reached me, reached me perhaps alone among my companions. It was, however, only through his books that I knew him, for I never met this famous author, who was by no means famous in Oxford at this time, being disregarded there and held of no account. Edmund Gosse once told me that when the memorial to Shelley was installed in University College, and a great gathering of the famous writers and eminent intellectuals of the land were assembled to be present at the unveiling of this monument, he himself had gone to Oxford and had suggested that Walter Pater should give him luncheon. Pater entertained him with his usual grave amenity; and when luncheon was finished, and Gosse suggested that it was time to join the others who were to be present at the ceremony, Pater told him where to go, but said that he himself could not accompany him as he was not among those who had received an invitation to attend.

In Balliol, indeed, the name of Pater was known, but it was only mentioned with contempt. Pater had been an early pupil of Jowett's; they had read Plato together; and I have always believed, though I have no proofs to give, that it was Jowett who had advised Pater to give up the writing of verse, to which he was greatly addicted, and try to become a writer of good prose. But when this effort resulted in the publication of Pater's *Renaissance*, Jowett took alarm at once.

While all melts under our feet, we may well catch at any exquisite passion, or any contribution to knowledge that seems by a lifted horizon to set the spirit free for a moment, or any stirring of the senses, strange dyes, and curious odours, or work of the artist's hands, or the face of one's friend . . .

To burn always with this hard, gemlike flame, to maintain this ecstasy, is success in life.

So Pater chanted from Brasenose in his magic rhythms, but his view of things was not acceptable in Balliol. To maintain an ecstasy, to burn with a hard gemlike flame, was by no means the Balliol conception of triumphant achievement. To beat New College in the Schools, to maintain a good place on the river, to win All Souls Fellowships and brilliant places in the Civil Service and high official honours, was more consonant with their ideal. No doubt this was the wiser view; no doubt the efficiency, wisdom, and justice which on the whole rule the counsels of the British Empire are in no inconsiderable part due to the moral, manly influence of Balliol.

It is not surprising, therefore, that not long before I went to Balliol the Master had felt himself called upon to mark, in an almost public manner, his disapprobation of Pater and all his ways; and it was only much later, when Pater published his wise and beautiful book on *Plato and Platonism*, that Jowett modified the harshness of his earlier judgement.

For the rest, I shared in that Oxford life which, in its setting of old colleges and gardens and little rivers, is surely the happiest and most enchanting life that is possible to young mortals. A taste of Paradise, a bit of the old golden world – so it seemed to me after my emancipation from that ogre's den in America. I had not known that life could hold such happiness, such enchanting talks and friendships, such kindness and good-fellowship – and I drank to the full from the enchanted cup. My literary ambitions, if they could be called ambitions, though not forgotten, were in abeyance for the time; my business was to get an education, and though I was acquainted with the budding authors who were at Oxford with me, – Lionel Johnson, Laurence Binyon, and

Max Beerbohm, – I did not become intimate with any of them; I was contented with the society I found in my own college. This society was made up, for the most part, of young men who belonged to the Whig political families, the Russells, the Carlisle Howards, and the Peels, who were destined to careers in the world of politics. I too became engaged in political activities; I used to speak at village meetings and work for Liberal candidates at by-elections; I joined the Oxford Charity Organization Committee; I organized meetings for temperance and social propaganda; and I think I was best known in Oxford as belonging to the not very estimable type of social reformer who combines extreme democratic views with no very pronounced dislike of the society of lords. In the dim anecdotal atmosphere of old-fashioned Oxford common rooms, where stories are elaborately related over the port wine and the walnuts, I have reason to believe that dialogues were invented between me and two American young ladies who were supposed to be studying in Oxford, in which perambulators were referred to as 'push-buggies', and spittoons were much discussed under the name of 'cuspidors'.

PARIS

——— ❋ ———

PARIS welcomes would-be artists with its urbane, heartless grace; it provides them with every facility for learning the art they will never learn to practise; it appropriates with a charming smile the savings they have brought with them, and with the same smile it watches them fade away or perish, knowing that new generations will soon appear to occupy their little hotels and lodgings. All are doomed, as Paris knows, to inevitable failure, but it goes on with its own business, remunerated and undisturbed.

Every year these art students arrive out of the darkness like flights of birds; they rejoice for brief or longer periods in the Paris sunshine, and then they disappear, and what becomes of them no one knows or cares. Do they return to their original homes, to teach art in provincial art schools and to paint the portraits of local magnates, or do they simply moulder away and die? Nobody, as I say, knows or cares.

The immense forgathering, as if drawn by some irresistible magnet, of æsthetic Americans in Paris was remarkable as a mass phenomenon, but the individuals who composed that mass, though I lived among them for a while, I did not find interesting. They had come to Paris from almost every region of my native country at who knows what sacrifice to themselves and to their parents, to study art; but in art itself they seemed to take hardly any interest – they almost never visited the Louvre, nor did they discuss any of the great masterpieces of European painting. Their talk was all of their own or each other's pictures and of the little twopenny shows where they were to be seen on exhibition. These pictures, painted with elaborate pains, were all alike, all imitative of each other; the narrow space of their little shows was filled with a vast, an almost intolerable monotony. Most interesting among these American students I found the indomitable old ladies who, released by the happy demise of their husbands and the maturity of their children, had escaped at last, at the age of seventy, perhaps, or even eighty, to realize their dreams of studying art in Paris. But these old ladies, whom one would see seated in their prim bonnets in the art schools, industriously making drawings of huge and naked males, all painted the same picture as their young contemporaries; it was not possible to distinguish among them. And yet no generalization is ever absolutely true. From among the thousands of indistinguishable art students of our race had emerged the American Whistler, the Englishman Sickert, and the Australian Charles Conder. Of these Whistler and Conder were then living in Paris.

On leaving Oxford, I had rented for twenty pounds a year a charming apartment – three rooms looking on a great cherry tree in a little garden – in the curious, shabby, provincial, yet cosmopolitan, Montparnasse quarter of Paris, with its little shops, its vast mysterious convents, its broad boulevards close by. It so happened that Whistler had his studio almost round the corner, and I often saw him either at this studio or at the charming pavilion where he lived with his English wife in the garden of an aristocratic hotel not far off. Whistler was then engaged in what was for him the almost interminable process of painting a portrait – the subject was the Comte de Montesquieu. This nobleman (whom Proust afterwards made famous) was depicted in an aristocratic pose, standing with a fur coat on his arm, and could not be expected to give the almost innumerable sessions which Whistler demanded of his subjects; but I could be easily called in to act as his substitute in certain aspects of his appearance. I was, like him, tall and slim, and could competently stand there with what was the principal feature of the picture, the fur coat flung across the arm. I was pleased to oblige the great painter, I was delighted to enjoy his company and watch him paint; but the task was one of the most arduous I have ever undertaken. Whistler had not the slightest pity for his subjects; art was something sacred, and the sufferings of those in its service were a matter of complete indifference to him. If, when he had finished his portraits of his sitters, they should all perish, what could that have mattered to the world? From the point of view of eternity, there is much to be said for this attitude of the artist. Of what interest or importance to us now are all their models? They are now all dust, and, as Donne would have pointed out, dust that is no longer even capable of emitting an evil odour. Why should we bother ourselves about them?

But to die in the effort to make immortal the fur coat of a stranger seemed to me a somewhat excessive sacrifice; and when I had stood until I felt I should die if I stood there longer, and would beg for a little rest or some change of position, 'In a moment, in just a moment,' Whistler would cheerfully answer, and then would go on painting. His method, as I observed it, was first of all to arrange his subject with incredible pains and care, so that every detail was to his liking, and to paint it with infinite touches and retouches; and then, when it seemed finished and perfect in execution, to stand back, gaze at it, and cry 'Ha!' and rush at it in a kind of fury and paint the whole thing out. It was like an actor rehearsing a part over and over again till he gets it perfect; the final performance, which may take a minute, has been preceded by many hours of rehearsal. This was the case, I think, even with Whistler's life-size protraits. The actual painting of each, as we now see it, was performed in the briefest of periods, but these had been preceded by an almost infinite number of rehearsals.

Such at least were my reflections as I stood till I almost dropped, bearing on my arm the Count's fur coat, which would be painted again and again with exquisite care in every detail, then again and again be painted out. But all things have an end, and at last respite would come. Whistler would abandon his brushes, and we would sit down to an entertainment which consisted not only in a delicious luncheon, but in talk as amusing as any I have ever heard. Whistler was not only incomparable as a wit (his *Gentle Art of Making Enemies* is proof enough of that), but he had accumulated (and I think repolished by frequent repetition) a long series of anecdotes concerning his life in England, in which every person of distinction, every institution of importance with which he had come into contact in that country, was made more ridiculous than words can say.

Self-important people, who take themselves seriously, have always worn for me a slightly comic aspect, and Whistler's mockery of the official side of English institutions I found extremely amusing. Outside of his art I did not regard him as a person deserving of much estimation. The record of his quarrels is more funny than edifying, and he was too fond of publicity and self-advertisement for my taste. But these failings hardly matter in a painter who, with regard to his painting, possessed a conscience of the utmost delicacy, and a sense of honour surpassing all I have ever known or heard of in what is after all perhaps the most honourable of all the arts. To do anything second-rate for money, or any kind of personal or social advantage, would never have been possible to Whistler; and though at times there was a touch in him of the loud, bar-frequenting American, his taste in matters of art was infallible and exquisite; he loved his paintings, and I think he could have told at any moment in what gallery or private collection even the most insignificant of them could be found. The paint brush was his appropriate weapon, and I remember once, when he was writing a series of outrageous letters, Mrs Whistler's remarking that Jimmy would be all right if he could only be kept from the inkpot.

HUNTING FOR MANUSCRIPTS

———— ✳ ————

E NGLAND has become the home of sport for many Americans, who come annually to this island for deer stalking, for fishing, and for the hunting of foxes. But there is another form of hunting which has occupied a good deal of my English leisure – the hunting, namely, for manuscripts of literary interest in English archives and old English country houses. I acquired my taste for this form of sport when I began to write the life of the old poet and ambassador and Provost of Eton, Sir Henry Wotton; and I spent some years in collecting his unpublished letters. The archives of the Record Office, the British Museum, and the Bodleian Library are easily accessible, and there are officials at these institutions ready and even eager to assist students in their labours. But I soon became aware that distinguished biographers preferred to make use of printed sources rather than to pursue their researches among unpublished papers. I found that since Walton's biography at least seven sketches, portraits, and lives of Wotton have been written by scholars of distinction, including Adolphus Ward and Sir Sidney Lee, but that none of these had looked at his dispatches, of which at least five hundred were preserved unread in the Record Office, or at his letters to be found in the British Museum. All these were, of course, easily accessible; one had only to ask for the packet which might contain a document of interest, and the packet would be brought to one's reading desk by a polite official.

When, however, I wished to pursue my hunting into the archives of private houses, I found that a much more elaborate method of procedure was required. It is quite useless, in my experience, to write out of the blue, so to speak, to great personages and ask permission to examine their muniments rooms and inherited manuscripts. Either they will not reply, or they will send curt refusals. I think that they do not know themselves (not being literate people) what treasures they possess; or if they do, they regard an unknown inquirer as a thief or gangster, with robbery as the object of his visit. I found it necessary, therefore, to procure some kind of personal introduction before writing to them. The plan I adopted was that of inquiring among the people I happened to meet if any of them knew, or knew anything about, the magnate whose manuscripts I wanted to examine; and once a personal relation of this kind was formed, however tenuous, all difficulties would at once vanish.

The world allots but meagre rewards to researchers; it allows them in recompense, however, the privilege of describing the discoveries they have made, and of thus enjoying what is one of the least reprehensible forms of human vanity – a form of self-glory not very amiable denominated by the inglorious term of 'boasting'. Undeterred, however, by that epithet, I shall avail myself of the scholar's licence – a licence also shared by anglers – by mentioning a few of my successes in this special sport.

In examining the Seventh Report of the Historical Manuscripts Commission, I found a note by A. J. Horwood, who had been sent in 1878 to examine the manuscripts, at a great mansion near Oakham, of a manuscript volume which contained 'copies of letters seemingly by and to Sir Henry Wotton'. I found that this house was in the possession of a certain elderly colonel, and I began inquiring among the people I met if any of them knew him. At last I met an old lady who was his cousin, and who kindly said that I might write to him and make use of her name as an introduction. I therefore wrote, and received a most courteous answer from the colonel, saying that he knew nothing of the manuscript book, and did not believe he possessed it, but that he was quite willing for me to come and look for it myself.

I thereupon went to Oakham, and took a cab up to an immense Italian villa, which is one of the biggest houses in England, if not the biggest. I drove into a great colonnaded courtyard of about twenty acres (larger, I believe, than the Great Court of Trinity College, Cambridge), and up to the splendid steps of the mansion – steps partially broken and partially overgrown with weeds, for the whole place looked ill-kept and considerably out of repair, as if funds were not abundant on that hilltop. I rang the great resounding front-door bell, and the stately portal was opened by an old gentleman in a shawl, who reminded me of the Duke of Wellington in his appearance. I introduced myself, and mentioned his cousin, of whom we talked awhile, and then I stated my errand, at which he gave a somewhat malicious chuckle and showed me into an immense library, which occupied one wing of the great house and looked about a mile long. It was full of debris, pictures without frames, frames without pictures, old rocking-horses without heads, and was lined with immense old bookshelves, reaching to ceilings that seemed to touch the sky. 'Now you can have a look, and you must let me give you luncheon later,' he said, and then he disappeared.

It was a cold day in November; the library was unheated, and I felt the beginnings of a violent cold upon me. My despair at the gigantic search in prospect (which would have required weeks at least for its satisfactory performance) can be imagined; but still I felt that, having come so far, I must take at least a look. While I was doing this, I happened to see the colonel with two maiden ladies (whom I after-wards found to be his daughters) staring at me through an immense window from the terrace outside. By great good fortune I found within half an hour the book I was looking for, and saw at once that it was of even greater interest than I had hoped, as it contained copies of many of Wotton's unpublished letters, a number of documents concerning his first embassy at Venice (1604–1610), and a large collection of notes of 'table-talk', kept by someone in his household at Venice during that period, with many anecdotes about Queen Elizabeth, James I, Henry IV, Bacon and Essex, and various personages of the time, as well as a number of poems by Donne and others, a copy of Donne's *Paradoxes*, with a long unpublished letter which Donne sent with them, and a number of other early unpublished letters by Donne, some signed and some unsigned, all of which had escaped Horwood's notice when he examined the manuscript.

I took the book to the colonel's study, where there was a good fire, and where the old gentleman sat reading *The Times*. Occasionally I caught his eye, staring at me over its pages as if he were asking himself what sort of creature I could be to take so great an interest in old papers.

When at last I hinted that it would take me more than an afternoon to master and copy out the contents of this volume, he most kindly asked me to come and pay him a visit for this purpose. I was, of course, delighted to accept this invitation, and spent several days in this great seventeenth-century palace, whose wide terraces overlooked perhaps the most famous of English hunting countries. I had my meals with the colonel and his daughters, and attended divine service with them in the chapel of the house. They all treated me with the perfect courtesy of their class, and made no attempt to find out who I was, or what motive had induced me to engage in this (to them) so incomprehensible a form of sport. They were much too polite to ask any questions.

When I found that the period of my visit was insufficient for an adequate study of the contents of this book, I arranged for the Oxford Press to purchase its copyright, and to have the volume sent to Oxford for careful copies to be made. Sir Herbert Grierson came to Oxford to examine the poems, which he afterwards published in his masterly edition of Donne's poems. I remember that when he and I were shut up together to examine this volume in a big room at the top of the Clarendon Press, Satan tempted me to make the suggestion that it would be rather fun to insert among these perfectly unknown notes of table-talk some chance remark about Bacon as a playwright which might set the Baconians agog; and I remember Grierson's expression of horror at this suggestion, which it is indeed lucky we didn't carry out, since, shortly after the volume was returned to the place where I had found it, the house was burnt down and the manuscript destroyed.

I published the letters of Wotton and the table-talk (with which, I need hardly say, I did not tamper) in my Life of Wotton. The letters of Donne (which were of great interest) were published by Mrs Simpson in her *Study of the Prose Works of John Donne*, and reprinted by John Hayward in the Nonesuch Donne.

Some years later, when Mrs Toynbee was editing Horace Walpole's letters, and I happened to be specially interested in Walpole at the time, I wrote to her (although I did not know her) saying that I hoped she would print more of Walpole's letters to Madame du Deffand, since the extracts from them published by Miss Berry seemed to me of such interest and merit. She replied that she would gladly do so, but that the box containing the Walpole–du-Deffand correspondence had not been traced since its sale at Strawberry Hill in 1842, and that no one knew where it was. Encouraged, I suppose, by a series of other successes in hunting for manuscripts in country houses, I replied with a rashness which now seems to me preposterous that I would find that box for her if she would tell me all she knew about it. She replied that it was supposed to have been bought at Strawberry Hill by a man of Asiatic origin named Dyce-Sombre, and that nothing had been heard of it since.

I looked up the history of the purchaser of this box, and found that it was an extraordinary one. His great-grandfather was a German carpenter, who went to India in 1754, and, becoming a soldier in the service of several native princes, acquired the appellation of Sombre – from his serious cast of countenance – instead of his German name Reinhard, and was given by the emperor of Delhi the principality of Sirdhama. This passed on his death to his wife, a dancing girl, who became the Begum of that state. Sombre in the meantime had begotten by a concubine a son called Zuffer yah Khan. Zuffer Khan died, leaving a daughter, who married George Alexander Dyce, the commandant of the Begum's forces. The son by this marriage inherited half a million sterling from the Begum at her decease, and added the name of Sombre to that of Dyce. He became a Roman Catholic, and was created by the Pope a chevalier of the Order of Christ, in consideration of the very large gifts the Begum had made to his Holiness.

In 1838, Dyce-Sombre came to England, where he married the daughter of an English peer. He entered Parliament and then a lunatic asylum, and died in 1851; and his wife, from whom he had been long separated, married a man of fortune who was afterwards created a peer under the title of Lord F. His title and estate were inherited by his son.

It was with this Begum's money that the desired box had been purchased; and I had a feeling, what is called a 'hunch', that the box was now in the possession, and reposed in the country house, of Lord F.

I cannot account for this hunch, but it amounted to so strong a conviction that I began again my tedious process of trying to establish some sort of relation with this backwoods peer, who lived in Staffordshire, and of whom no one I met seemed to have ever heard. At last I met in Florence a young man who told me that this Lord F. was the intimate friend of his cousin, the Dean of York, and suggested that I should write to the Dean, saying that he had told me I might do so. This suggestion I adopted; and after making inquiries as to how a letter to a Dean should be properly addressed, I sent a polite epistle to the Very Reverend gentleman (who I found was himself a man of letters, having written a book on *The Heraldry of York Minster*). I received a most courteous reply from the Dean, who said yes, Lord F. was his friend, and that I had better write to him, telling him that he (the Dean) had told me to do so. I thereupon wrote to Lord F., delicately suggesting that the Dean of York was a great pal of mine, and asking him if he happened to possess among his archives this box from Strawberry Hill.

Thereupon I waited for some weeks, perhaps a month or two, but received no answer. Then came a letter from Mrs Toynbee, reminding me that I had agreed to find these letters, and telling me that she was holding up her edition of Walpole for them; and well, so to speak, what about it? I sat down and wrote a letter of apology to the irritated lady, saying that I had been far too presumptuous in making this promise, in which I regretted to say that I had completely failed.

I was living at High Buildings at the time, and used to walk to the village post office every day to get my letters. Before dropping my letter to Mrs Toynbee in the box, I opened one addressed to me, which turned out to be from Lord F. himself, in which he wrote, with many apologies, to say that he had mislaid my note and had only come on it that morning; whereupon he had gone up to his attic and had found there the box about which I had written, and which he had had no notion that he possessed. It would be, he feared, of no interest to me, as he had found, on examining the letters in it, that some autograph collector had cut off the signatures from them. However, he politely added, if I cared to come to Staffordshire, he would put the box at my disposal, to make any use I wished of its contents. He ended with messages of regard to our common friend, the Dean of York. I tore up my first letter, therefore, to Mrs Toynbee, and went home to write another to her, in which I said that, having promised to find this box, I had, of course, done so, and that it was now in Lord F.'s attic in Staffordshire, and if she would write to him, mentioning my name and that of the Dean of York, he would no doubt put it at her disposal.

Thereupon Mrs Toynbee (with, I think, her husband, Paget Toynbee) went leaping up to Staffordshire, and found that the box contained even greater treasures than she could have hoped for – hundreds and hundreds of unpublished letters from Madame du Deffand, who was only second in fame as a letter writer to Madame de Sévigné. They were all annotated (evidently for publication) by Horace Walpole himself, and among them were a certain number of Walpole's own letters, though he seems to have destroyed most of them on account of the bad French in which he believed that they had been written. Mrs Toynbee spent some years in preparing a scholarly edition of these manuscripts, and this edition was published in three big volumes, after her death, by her husband.

I confess that my angler's vanity was a little hurt by the fact that no copy of this book was sent to me, and that my share in this catch was not referred to. This, however, may have been due to the fact that Mrs Toynbee was dead when her husband brought out the book.

My last experience of this sport I should like to put on record – not that I have any grievance to air, but because I think it may prove one day of interest to literary historians. I happened to see last year in David Alec Wilson's portentous life of Carlyle a statement that Carlyle's letters to the second Lord Ashburton were in the possession of a certain noble marquis, now deceased. Again that voice told me that his family had somewhere in their possession the whole Carlyle–Ashburton correspondence. So I began trying to find someone who was acquainted with them; and at last a lady who was a friend of mine told me that she knew them very well, and promised to ask when she next saw them whether they had these letters. Not long after she wrote to say that she had inquired, and that they said they didn't have them and knew nothing about them. I replied that I thought her noble friends might do well to have another look, as one letter at least had been seen not long ago by Carlyle's biographer. Shortly afterwards I received a note which I first thought was the rudest, and then saw was one of the kindest I had ever received from one of these noble but unlettered personages, who so curiously combine incivility to strangers with generosity and courtesy to anyone who may seem to have some connection with anyone of their class.

The letter was addressed to 'Mr (or Mrs) L. P. Smith', and, beginning 'Dear Sir or Madam', stated that the writer had received two scrawls from my friend, neither of which he could read, and so thought it better to write to me direct. He had, he said, the Carlyle letters, but they were of a distinctly personal nature, being addressed to members of his family now deceased. He had looked at them, but could not see that they possessed any interest; however, he would be delighted to lend me typewritten copies of them, if I would undertake to submit to him any extracts from them before I made use of them for publication.

I of course answered that I should be very glad to see these copies, and I offered to pay to have them made. No notice was taken of this offer; and in a few months I received a heap of typewritten copies of the Carlyle correspondence – 256 letters of Carlyle's, 27 of Mrs Carlyle's, and other documents concerning the relations of the Carlyles and the Ashburtons, all of them unpublished. Of Carlyle's letters 121 were to the first Lady Ashburton (Lady Harriet Baring), 94 to the second, and 41 to Lord Ashburton, the whole correspondence covering a period of thirty-four years.

I found them very interesting reading – Carlyle being to my mind one of the best of letter writers, and Mrs Carlyle, of course, always fascinating. Carlyle was at his best in writing to the Barings. The letters to Lady Harriet show that he was considerably bewitched by this great lady, and that Mrs Carlyle had some reason to be jealous. Her successor, Louisa, Lady Ashburton, was of a very different character, and proved herself to be the good angel of Carlyle, and also of Mrs Carlyle, with whom she formed a most devoted friendship. She too was a clever woman, who, after the death of her husband, became engaged to Robert Browning. But she broke off the engagement, to his great indignation, and he is supposed to have written the famous lines to her:

> Would it were I had been false, not you!
> I that am nothing, not you that are all:
> I, never the worse for a touch or two
> On my speckled hide.

The owner of these letters wrote me that I could take extracts from them, but that he would reserve the right of refusing, even at the last moment, to allow any extract to be printed. The whole correspondence he would not permit to be published, as he didn't want to have anyone making money out of the friendships of his relations. I did not feel like undertaking any publication under the supervision of this kind, but arbitrary and unlettered, nobleman. I therefore returned them to him, with due thanks for letting me see them, and they are still in his possession. I feel that a book ought sometime to be made of them, since the friendship of the Carlyles with the Ashburtons was the most important friendship of their lives, and in writing to all three of them both the Carlyles wrote their best. Through friends and relations of the owner of these manuscripts I have made several attempts to obtain permission for such a volume to be edited and published by some competent person, but so far my efforts have been in vain. But one day no doubt these letters will see the light. They will make a volume full of good reading and of important literary interest.

Only the other day I had a queer experience, and thought for a moment that I had heard that plaguy Voice again. I was sitting at luncheon by a lady who is a scholar of repute, and, speaking of manuscripts, she told me that her first job was to catalogue the manuscripts and books at Gorhambury for the Lord Verulam of the time. She said that in poking about, somewhat indiscreetly, in an old cupboard, she had found, under a heap of rubbish, a number of old playbills of Shakespeare's plays. She found that in fact her search had been an indiscretion; Lord Verulam did not want anything to be known about these playbills, as he had been much bothered by Baconian cranks and did not care to have them after him again.

Playbills of Shakespeare's age are, I believe, unknown, and that bills of some of Shakespeare's plays should be found in the home of Bacon's heir seemed to me a suggestion full of disagreeable possibilities, but one which perhaps it was my duty as a scholar to follow up. On writing, however, to the lady in question, I received the following reassuring reply:

Yes, I really did say we found Shakespearean playbills at Gorhambury in 1911 or thereabouts – but while old they were far from being contemporary. They would be waste of a scholar's time – if they still exist – but would in those days have provided a lot of healthy exercise for a Baconian Heretic.

In this sport of hunting for manuscripts in English country houses, either I have had extraordinary luck, or else such houses are full of treasures for those who will take the trouble to hunt for them. But it is necessary to acquire the technique of pursuing this form of chase – a form, to my mind, superior in interest to that of fishing for big fish or of hunting foxes. And there are not only letters to reward the hunters. In the last year or two a manuscript of the first literary importance has been discovered in an old country house, *The Book of Marjorie Kempe*, a frank autobiography written in the most vivid and enchanting style, and full of incredible avowals. It is by centuries the earliest autobiography in English, and indeed a great open window into the life of the early fifteenth century.

Commonplace books full of contemporary verse abound also in old libraries, which have never been examined by persons with a taste for poetry of merit. Many Elizabethans wrote beautiful poems which they never thought of printing, but circulated among their friends, who made copies of them. I have already mentioned the beautiful unpublished verses in the volume of Wotton's letters which I found, some of which have appeared in recent anthologies. The only other volume I know of which has been examined from the point of view of literary merit is the volume, now famous, in the Christ Church library, in which poems were found of surpassing beauty that have become permanent additions to our treasure of Elizabethan poetry.

PART II: CRITICAL WRITINGS

1: 'Four Romantic Words'

from

Words and Idioms:
Studies in the English Language (1925)

FOUR ROMANTIC WORDS

——— ✳ ———

I

I MENTIONED in the previous chapter, among the English words borrowed into foreign languages, one adjective, the word *romantic*, which has been added to all the vocabularies of Europe. This is a word of such prime importance that, to give an account of its origin, and its adventures, both in England and abroad, a separate study will be necessary. There is no word in our language which has a more 'romantic' history; much in its signification, both as we employ it now and as we find it employed in our elder literature, is the result of what it has been through; and a knowledge of all this will be of assistance in enabling us to understand the various thoughts and ways of feeling which it has come to express, and which still deeply colour its meaning. But the emergence of the word *romantic* is not an isolated phenomenon; its history is closely connected with the history of several other terms of modern aesthetic criticism – terms which came into use at about the same time, and shared the same adventures. This cluster of romantic words is the product of one of the most important movements of modern thought, and the history of that movement is curiously mirrored in their usage. They are, both in formation and meaning, very largely of English origin; from English they made their way into foreign languages; and the new conceptions they express form one of the most notable of English contributions to European thought.

Of this cluster of new terms, or of old terms endowed with new meanings, the earliest to make its appearance is the adjective *romantic*, of which the first instance is given in the *Oxford Dictionary* under the date of 1659.[1] It is apparently a word of English origin,[2] formed from the English word *romant* or *romaunt* – a word which was borrowed in the sixteenth century from the French *romaunt*, and which, used as a variant of *romance* in the seventeenth century, was revived as an archaism in the nineteenth. Before, however, *romantic* became a

93

current term, a number of other attempts were made, as the *Oxford Dictionary* shows us, to form adjectives with the same meaning. In 1653 Dorothy Osborne writes of a *romance* squire, and in the following year of a *romance* story; in 1656 the Duchess of Newcastle speaks of her '*Romancicall* Tales'; and we also find the adjectives *romancial* (1653) and *romancy* (1654). The fact that all these adjectives crop up in the seven years between 1653 and 1659, and that *romantic* soon becomes a current term, is certainly curious. Why just at this time was there a need felt for this adjective which had never been felt before?

The emergence of a new term to describe a certain phenomenon, of a new adjective to designate a certain quality, is always of interest, both linguistically and from the point of view of the history of human thought. That history would be a much simpler matter (and language, too, a much more precise instrument) if new thoughts on their appearance, and new facts at their discovery, could at once be analysed and explained and named with scientific precision. But even in science this seldom happens; we find rather that a whole complex group of facts, like those for instance of gas or electricity, are at first somewhat vaguely noticed, and are given, more or less by chance, a name like that of *gas*, which is an arbitrary formation, or that of *electricity*, which is derived from the attractive power of *electrum* or amber when rubbed – the first electric phenomenon to be noticed. *Gas*, *electric*, and *electricity* are what Dr Bradley called 'identifying' words;[3] sometimes, however, a new discovery is given a 'descriptive' name like *gravitation*; or again, as with *oxygen*, an explanatory word may be formed which attempts more adequately to account for the new phenomenon. But comprehension is reached, if indeed it is ever reached, long after recognition; analytic and explanatory terms for half-understood phenomena often imply, like *oxygen* ('generator of acids'), a false explanation; the usual, and much the safest way, is to give a non-committal, designating, or at most a descriptive name to a new experience, which then, gradually, and in the course of time, can be more accurately defined and perhaps at last explained. In the even more elusive phenomena of aesthetic perceptions, this process of identification, denotation, and suggested explanation is still more tentative and slow; new aspects of thought and feeling come to be designated by names which are at first little more than the chance names of vague impressions – obscure perceptions of some quality for which a label of some kind would be convenient. This label then forms a centre of attraction for other vague perceptions which group themselves about it; and it is only by a long and tentative process of collective thought that the various aspects of the phenomena described become more apparent, and the label or name acquires more definite meanings. Our word *romantic* is a conspicuous instance of this process. Its appearance in the middle of the seventeenth century is an indication of a change in human thought, and marks the moment when that change had become obvious enough to need a term to express it. *Romantic*, like *romancy* and *romancical*, simply meant 'like the old romances', and shows that men at this time were becoming aware of certain qualities in these romances for which they needed a name – that they were becoming critical of them, and had begun to view them with a certain detachment. These romances were of two kinds: there were the medieval tales of chivalry and knight-errants, of 'The Palmerins of England and the Amadises of Gaul' who, as Hazlitt describes them, 'made their way to their mistresses' hearts by slaying giants and taming dragons'; and there were also those prolix French romances of intrigue and gallantry, which succeeded the earlier tales. The special characteristic of all these romances, for which a name was now needed, was their falseness and unreality, all that was imaginary and impossible in them, all that was contrary to the more rational view of life which was beginning to dominate men's minds. The growth of this conception of 'order' and 'nature', this 'dawn of reason', as an eighteenth-century writer called it, threw into relief certain groups of irrational elements which were opposed to it. The phenomena of religious fanaticism were branded as *enthusiasm*, and the fictions and imaginations of the old romances were labelled by the word *romantic*. The meaning of 'false', 'fictitious', 'imaginary', implied by *romantic* was applied both to the supernatural elements in the medieval romances, their giants, magicians, and enchanted castles; and also to the false, impossible, high-flown sentiments of the later romances; those 'wild romantic tales', as a seventeenth-century writer described them, 'wherein they strain love and honour to that ridiculous height that it becomes burlesque.'[4]

Both these elements, the supernatural and what we now call the sentimental, were falling into disrepute at the time when the word *romantic* appeared to describe them. In 1650 Hobbes, in that famous answer to Davenant, which formed the basis of neo-classical criticism in England, protested against the use of the supernatural, against fiction that exceeded the possibility of 'Nature', 'impenetrable armour, Inchanted Castles, invulnerable bodies, Iron Men, Flying horses';[5] and his protest was echoed by the critics who followed after him; while Sir William Temple[6] pointed out how Cervantes had turned into ridicule 'the Romantick Honour and Love'[7] of the romances of chivalry.

In the course of the next hundred and fifty years the word *romantic*, as a description of false and fictitious beings and feelings, without real existence in fact or in human nature, fell more and more into disrepute and disestimation. The particular shade of meaning given to a word, the special nuance of feeling it expresses, can often be best seen by the company it keeps; and in the writings of this period we find the word *romantic* coupled with terms like 'chimerical', 'ridiculous', 'unnatural', 'bombast'; we read of 'childish and romantic poems', of 'romantic absurdities and incredible fictions': 'can anything', Bishop South asks, 'be imagined more profane and impious, absurd and indeed romantic?' and Psalmanazar confesses to the 'vile and romantic' deception of his pretence to be a native of Formosa.

It was the need, therefore, to mark the contrast between the truth of nature and the falsehood of romance which first brought into use this famous adjective. It makes its appearance at the moment when as an eighteenth-century writer puts it, 'reason was but dawning, as we may say, and just about to gain the ascendant over the portentous spectres of the imagination. Its growing splendour, in the end, put them all to flight.'[8] Bishop Hurd is writing of what he calls the 'romantic' literature of the Elizabethan age, which, according to him was haunted by these spectres: the growing splendour which banished them was that of the Age of Reason, the *Éclaircissement*, the *Aufklärung* – that conception of order and truth, of the whole universe governed by law, which rose in the latter half of the seventeenth century like a sunrise of reason over the spectre-haunted Europe, with its romantic literature, its superstitions, its fanaticisms, and its religious wars.

Of all periods in the history of poetry perhaps the one which is most external to our sympathies, opaque and impenetrable to our imaginations, is precisely this period which lies so near us in the point of time, this Age of Reason, with its bewigged platitudes, its shallow criticism, and its intolerably didactic verse. How can the most practised amateur of historical emotions read Pope's *Essay on Man* with the enthusiasm which carried that sententious poem over Europe, or feel the disgust which was aroused, as Evelyn noted,[9] in that 'refined age', by plays like *Hamlet*? To recapture that mood, to bathe again in the freshness of that dawn, is not permitted to us; but perhaps, in the architecture of the period, in the severe beauty of some classical church or mansion, with its ornaments adorning, like noble rhetoric, its perfect proportions and ordered forms, we can best realize the charm of the qualities of order and reason and correctness, which were then prized and sought for, not only in architecture, but in poetry as well.

The literary revolution of this period was well summed up by Thomas Warton, when he said that a poetry succeeded the elder poetry in which 'imagination gave way to correctness'.[10] The connection between poetry and Imagination or Fancy (the distinction between these two terms was not established till much later) was often alluded to by sixteenth-century writers; but it would be vain to seek in the psychology and criticism of that time any clear definition of the meaning of the term *imagination*, which had been introduced into Latin as a translation of the Greek φαντασία, and which the Renaissance had inherited from Scholastic philosophy. Notions, however, which are now more definite to our minds were then held as it were in solution; Bacon divided the human understanding into three faculties, referring history to Memory, philosophy to Reason, and poesy to Imagination;[11] and Shakespeare expressed this connection in words which have a strangely modern sound, when he wrote:

> The lunatic, the lover, and the poet
> Are of imagination all compact . . .
> And, as imagination bodies forth
> The forms of things unknown, the poet's pen
> Turns them to shapes, and gives to airy nothing
> A local habitation and a name.[12]

But with the growth of neo-classical criticism this large and indefinite meaning of imagination was narrowed and confined.

Hobbes's psychology, as Professor Spingarn has pointed out, became the groundwork of Restoration criticism, and to Hobbes the essential element in poetry was Reason. 'Judgement,' he wrote, 'begets the strength and structure, and Fancy begets the ornaments of a Poem.'[13] The imagination came to be regarded as *la folle du logis*, in Descartes' phrase, or, in Dryden's words, as a wild, lawless faculty, which was the begetter of madness, dreams, and fever, but which, held strictly subordinate to Reason, could be usefully employed in finding, in the field of memory, illustrations, metaphors, and other useful ornaments for the sound structure of Reason. Or, at the most, following what Longinus had said of φαντασία, the power was attributed to the imagination of making the poet seem to behold the very things he is describing, and thus enabling him to display them to the life before the reader's eyes. But, as Dryden wrote, quoting from the famous French critic Rapin, 'if this fancy be not regulated, it is a mere caprice, and utterly incapable to produce a reasonable and judicious poem.'[14]

The qualities designated by these critics as *romantic* were therefore the mere product of unregulated imagination;[15] they were not reasonable, they did not imitate Nature, and they were therefore condemned as Gothic, unnatural, ridiculous and childish. We can therefore understand Pope's boast:

> That not in Fancy's maze he wander'd long,
> But stoop'd to Truth, and moraliz'd his song.[16]

This theory of poetry was logical, consistent, and worthy of serious and judicious men, who, weary of wild conceits and ornaments and fantastic dreams, welcomed it with an enthusiasm which is difficult for us to share. But, like other theories of poetry, it did not correspond to the facts, and even in its heyday of triumph it began to collapse and crumble. A new way of looking at things began to grow up alongside it, based upon a greater appreciation of the value and importance of the imagination in works of art. With this gradual and only half-conscious shift of feeling, which began early in the eighteenth century in England, and flowered at last in the so-called Romantic Movement, the word *romantic* itself began to acquire fresh values and new meanings. It is no longer always used as a term of depreciation; Addison describes Milton's account of Thammuz as 'finely Romantic',[17] and Thomson speaks of a 'fine, romantic kind of melancholy'. The Gothic and romantic periods of history, the Middle Ages and the Elizabethan (for both these were regarded as Gothic and romantic), began to interest students; the old 'romantic' poet Spenser, and the old tales of adventure and magic, came again into favour, and *romantic* began to mean something which, though absurd, was captivating to the imagination.[18] Horace Walpole confessed that he preferred the 'romantic' scenes of the past,[19] and the Vicar of Wakefield tells, how owing to his wife's reading of romances, two 'romantic' names were given to his daughters.

In these usages of the English word *romantic*, the corresponding French adjective *romanesque* was a more or less exact equivalent, and is to be found in the early French translation of Pope's line:

If Folly grow romantic, I must paint it.[20]

But already, before the eighteenth century, another use had been found for the English word which *romanesque* did not translate. Along with its depreciatory use for the incidents and sentiments of the old romances, it was also used as an adjective of half-conscious appreciation for scenes and places like those which they describe. The adjective *romancy* or *romantic* was applied very early to the scenery of the neighbourhood of Wilton, where Sidney's *Arcadia* was composed. 'The Arcadia,' Aubrey wrote, 'is about Vernditch and Wilton, and these romancy plaines and boscages did no doubt conduce to the heightening of Sir Philip Sydney's phancie.'[21] In another place he speaks of his rides through this '*romantick* country', with its flocks of sheep and nut-brown shepherdesses;[22] and earlier, under the date of 1654, Evelyn notes in his *Diary*, 'Salisbury Plain reminded me of the pleasant lives of the shepherds we read of in romances.'[23] But the word is also used for buildings: in 1666 Pepys called Windsor Castle 'the most romantique castle that is in the world';[24] and even earlier, in 1654, Evelyn writes of a 'very romantic' country-seat on the side of a

99

'horrid Alp' near Bristol;[25] and under the date of 1679 he says, speaking of the Duke of Buckingham's country house at Clifden, 'The grotts in the chalky rock are pretty: 'tis a romantic object, and the place altogether answers the most poetical description that can be made of solitude, precipice, prospect, or whatever can contribute to a thing so very like their [the romancers'] imaginations.'[26] Sir William Temple wrote in his *Essay on Gardening* (1685) of the 'romantic palace' of Alcinous described by Homer; and Addison in his *Remarks on Italy* (1705) says that on his journey between Marseilles and Genoa he was shown in the distance 'The Deserts, which have been rendered so famous by the penance of Mary Magdalene who . . . is said to have wept away the rest of her life among these solitary rocks and mountains. It is so romantic a scene, that it has always probably given occasion to such chimerical relations.'[27] This use of the adjective in the description of places, meaning, as the *Oxford Dictionary* defines it, 'redolent or suggestive of romance; appealing to the imaginations and feelings,' became more current after 1711, when Addison, in his famous essay on the ballad of Chevy Chase in the *Spectator*, spoke of 'The fine romantic situation' of that battle.[28] Thomson writes in his *Seasons* of 'oaks romantic', of a 'romantic' mountain, of the 'romantic' Caledonian landscape. Mason writes of 'an old romantic forest';[24] and even Dr Johnson, who is not thought of as a romantic writer, and who almost invariably uses the word with its depreciatory meaning ('romantic and superfluous', 'ridiculous and romantic', 'romantic absurdities or incredible fictions', etc.), was so influenced by the prevalent fashion as to try his unwieldy hand at a landscape of this kind.

> When night overshadows a romantick scene, all is stillness, silence, and quiet; the poets of the grove cease their melody, the moon towers over the World in gentle majesty, men forget their labours and their cares, and every passion and pursuit is for a while suspended.[30]

The word *romantic* then, from the general meaning of 'like the old romances', came to be used as a descriptive term for the scenes which they describe, old castles, mountains and forests, pastoral plains, waste and solitary places. In the earlier instances of the adjective the literary reference is more or less explicit; but by the eighteenth century it had come to express more generally the newly awakened, but as yet half-conscious, love for wild nature, for mountains and moors, for 'the *Woods*, the *Rivers*, or *Sea-shores*', which Shaftesbury mentions as sought by those 'who are deep in this *romantick* way'.[31]

When English books of this period were translated into French, the translators either avoided the adjective in this usage, or rendered it by *romanesque* or *pittoresque*. *Romantick* or *romantique* is, however, found occasionally as a loan word from English;[32] about 1776 two French authors, one of them Letourneur, the translator of Shakespeare, and the other the Marquis de Girardin, the author of a book on landscape, made deliberate use of the word, giving in notes their reasons for borrowing this *mot Anglois*, as they called it. Monsieur A. François, in his brilliant essay on *Romantique*[33] – an essay from which much of my information about the French history of the word is derived – reprints these notes, and they are of great importance, proving, as they do, the English origin of the word, and explaining its meaning. It meant more, they said, than *romanesque* or *pittoresque: romanesque* meant 'chimerical', or 'fabulous', while *pittoresque* describes a scene that strikes the eye and arouses admiration. But *romantic* implies an appeal as well to the feelings and the imagination: it not only describes the scene, but 'the touching impression we receive from it'. Both authors enumerate the scenes that in the eighteenth century were considered romantic, the heaths, the sea, the clouds of the 'Caledonian landscape', mountains, torrents and waterfalls, and le *'lovely moon' des Anglois*. The word, M. François suggests, was probably brought to the notice of Rousseau by one of these authors, his friend Girardin; and it was finally given full rights of citizenship in the French language by Rousseau, when, in that incomparable masterpiece of his prose, his famous fifth *Rêverie du promeneur solitaire*, he wrote 'les rives du Lac de Bienne sont plus sauvages & romantiques que celles du Lac de Geneve.'[54] The word soon became fashionable in France, and was included in the Dictionary of the French Academy in 1798, with the definition, 'Il se dit ordinairement des lieux, des paysages, qui rappelent à l'imagination les descriptions des poëmes et des romans.'

These French definitions of *romantique* help us to a clear understanding of this special use of the word. Two points stand out clearly. In the first place *romantic* is, like *interesting, charming, exciting,* and many other adjectives, one of those modern words which describe, not so much the objective qualities of things, as our response to them, the feelings they arouse in the susceptible spectator. And secondly, if we examine the special subjective feeling described by *romantic,* we see that it is a literary emotion (as indeed the derivation of the word from *romant* implies); it is Nature seen through the medium of literature, through a mist of associations and sentiments derived from poetry and fiction. It is curious also to note the appearance and popularity of the word *picturesque* at the same time as *romantic;* for just as *romantic* means Nature seen through a literary medium, so *picturesque* was used to describe scenes that were like pictures, and were seen through the medium of another art, that of painting. Painting and literature had been from ancient times judged and criticized by their relation to Nature; but this curious reversal of the process, the projection of art into Nature, the contemplation of Nature through the coloured glass of art, and from a consciously literary or pictorial point of view, is an element that must not be neglected in any definition of the word we are discussing. It is a nice instance of those subtle changes in men's feelings, and in their ways of looking at the world, which are so important and yet so elusive, and which can perhaps be most definitely traced in the emergence of new terms, or in a change in the meaning of old ones.

Picturesque came by way of France to England from the country of painting, from Italy; but *romantic* is a word, as our Swiss critic remarks, deposited on French soil by those currents of English thought and feeling which had reached it in the eighteenth century. Growing out of the heart of old romance, the word had absorbed into its meaning the glamour and newly-discovered beauty of moonlight and moors and mountains; it had then travelled with the fashion for English gardens and the fame of Shakespeare to France, where, welcomed by the great apostle of Nature, Rousseau, it enriched the French language with a definite term for the feeling of which French-men had already become conscious in the presence of wild nature, and which they had hitherto expressed by the vague term *je ne sais quoi.*[35]

I have quoted the definition of *romantique* given by the Dictionary of the French Academy when the word was formally admitted into the French language: Littré in his dictionary of a later date (1869), after repeating this definition, adds to the word quite another meaning. 'It is used,' he says, 'of writers who emancipate themselves from the rules of composition and style established by the classical authors.' To explain how the word acquired this additional sense, it is necessary to follow its adventures in Germany, for it was in Germany that this meaning was added to it, and it only became current in France as a borrowing from German sources.

The English word *romantic* was borrowed into German, as into French, late in the seventeenth century, *romanhaft* being (like *romanesque*) an older term in that language. *Romantisch* appears in a translation of Thomson's *Seasons*; it was used by Herder to describe wild and uncultivated landscape, and also by Wieland in his famous line:

Zum Ritt ins alte Romantische Land.[36]

But the word was applied not only to the scenes and landscapes described in the romances, but also, following certain precedents which can be found in English criticism,[37] to the literature itself which describes these scenes. Romantic literature and poetry, the literature and poetry of the Middle Ages, were, in contrast with those of the classical times, called *romantisch*; and from this comparison and contrast the German philosophers and critics, as they pondered over it in their Teutonic cogitations, evolved that great bugbear of modern criticism, the famous opposition between 'classical and romantic'. Goethe took upon Schiller and himself the responsibility of having added to the world's woes this famous subject of debate;[38] 'the idea', he told Eckermann, 'of the distinction between classical and romantic poetry, which is now spread over the whole world, and occasions so many quarrels and divisions, came originally from Schiller and myself . . . The Schlegels took up this idea, and carried it further, so that it has now been diffused over the whole world; and every one talks about classicism and romanticism – of which nobody thought fifty years ago.'[39]

The word *romantic*, thus brought in Germany into opposition with the antagonistic term 'classical', became at the end of the eighteenth century the battle-cry of a school of wild poets and Catholic reactionaries. This war spread from Germany to France, the seeds of it being carried thither by that adventurous literary lady, Madame de Staël. It was her famous book *De l'Allemagne* (written with the assistance of A. W. Schlegel, who had done much to elucidate – or darken – the meaning of these terms) which brought to France the new meanings which the word *romantic* [40] had acquired in Germany; and there, inscribed once more on the banners of young poets, it waved in the van of those still more famous battles of French Romanticism about which the world has heard so much. From France the word returned to the home of its pastoral youth, [41] curiously changed and transformed by its foreign experiences, its adventures in the company of German Jesuits, German philosophers, and French radicals, and loaded with a whole new world of meanings.

In the antithesis between romanticism and classicism, worked out by German thinkers, there was thus an explosive element, which made the word *romantic* into a famous battle-cry; the term coming to designate, as we see by Littré's definition, those writers who were in rebellion against the classical rules of composition. The romantic poets, first in Germany and then in France, were the poets who, scorning and rejecting the models of the past and the received rules of composition, prided themselves on their freedom from law, and on their own artistic spontaneity. The origin and history of this aspect of Romanticism is of considerable interest, and has attracted much critical attention. It has not, however, been treated as yet from the point of view of lexicography, although the lexicographer can, I think, do something to elucidate that history. For this movement was already in possession of three other battle-cries before *Romantic* was inscribed upon its banners; and it will be necessary to give some account of these three terms in order to make clear its full meaning.

II

The first of these terms which I shall treat of is the great modern word *originality*. This word is derived of course from the adjective *original*, a word which has certain religious associations, since it is first found in English in the phrase 'original sin', but which, as a term of literary criticism, comes from the vocabulary of painting. It was easy to borrow from painting the distinction between an original picture and a copy; this distinction is found in literary criticism in the middle of the seventeenth century;[42] it was adopted by Dryden, who speaks of Shakespeare's Juliet and Desdemona as 'originals';[43] and it soon became a current term, especially with reference to Shakespeare, being authorized by Pope's famous sentence in his preface to Shakespeare's works, 'If ever any Author deserved the name of an *Original*, it was Shakespeare. Homer himself drew not his art so immediately from the fountains of Nature.' From the word *original* in its use as an adjective, a noun was formed, the abstract term *originality*,[44] to designate the quality of first-handedness in a work of art. All art, the early critics agreed, was imitation; but there were two kinds of imitation – the imitation of Nature (by Nature they meant very much what we mean by 'life'), and the imitation of other works of art. The imitation of Nature was original imitation: the writer who drew his materials from the observation of Nature was an original writer. The imitation of other artists was, as a critic of the earlier part of the eighteenth century said, 'the bane of writing', 'for Poetry, in this respect, resembles Painting; no Performance in it can be valuable, which is not an Original.'[45] Primary and original copying was called invention,[46] or finding (εὕρεσις); without invention, as Dryden, said, 'a painter is but a copier, and a poet but a plagiary of others';[47] invention in respect of the matter of a work of art was simply observation; though in respect to the form, the disposition and embellishing of the work were also called 'invention'. Originality was simply newness and truth of observation or invention. The great original poets, like Homer and Shakespeare, were those who had most directly imitated Nature, and given the richest and most profound renderings of what they found.

The term *invention*, which criticism had inherited from classical rhetoric, served for a long time as a name for that finding in Nature of something new to copy which was called *originality*. Invention was defined by Temple as 'the mother of poetry.' 'The first happiness of the poet's imagination,' Dryden wrote, 'is properly invention, or finding of the thought';[48] and, in his life of Milton, Dr Johnson, declared 'the highest praise of genius is original invention.'

This notion of primary copying, or 'invention', seems to have been regarded for some time as a satisfactory explanation of originality, and is repeated as late as Hazlitt, who said that 'Originality consists in seeing Nature for yourself.'[49] But even the earlier critics seem to have become vaguely aware that there were certain aspects of poetry for which the word *invention* was not quite an adequate description. For *invention* by its etymology meant 'finding'; it was primarily a process of observing and copying Nature – and yet was all poetry nothing more than an imitation and an adornment of Nature? Was there nothing more in an original author than fresh and primary observation? The date at which this imitation-theory first began to break down can be neatly fixed by the appearance of another term which was destined to replace the word *invention* in many of its uses. In the works of Shakespeare, who, it was agreed, was the most original writer of modern times, there was one element which, however much they might stretch the meaning of the word, could hardly be called an imitation of Nature. This element was the supernatural, the 'magical World of Spirits', the fairies, the witches and midnight ghosts, which seemed as living and real as the human beings in his plays. Dryden, faced with this difficulty, tried to justify the description of 'fairies, pigmies, and the extraordinary effects of magic', by saying that the poet was allowed the liberty of describing things which existed in popular belief (popular belief being part of 'Nature'), and thus Shakespeare's *Tempest* and his *Midsummer Night's Dream* were to be defended.[50] When, however, Dryden came to write of the character of Caliban, he seems to have felt that the imitation-theory, the theory that, as he put it, 'the poet dresses truth and adorns Nature, but does not alter them,' was stretched almost to the breaking-point. There was, he seems to have felt, a difference between 'drawing' characters which had existed, or might have existed in Nature – or which others had believed to exist – and representing a being like Caliban, 'a species of himself, begotten by an incubus on a witch', and yet with a person and a character of his own, and with a 'language as hobgoblin as his person'.

III

I put some emphasis on this passage in Dryden because it marks, however vaguely, a real turning-point in English criticism; and also because there slipped into Dryden's vocabulary in this passage about Caliban an alternative word for 'invented' which was destined to be echoed and repeated, and to acquire, in the process of time, a very great importance. 'Shakespeare,' he says, 'seems there to have created a person which was not in Nature, a boldness which, at first sight, would appear intolerable.'[51] Dryden was not the first writer to employ in literary criticism the word *create*, with its solemn religious associations,[52] but its use in this connection, before he gave it currency, was sporadic and unusual.[53] We find it, after Dryden, in the writings of Sir William Temple;[54] and Addison, who echoes much of Dryden's criticism, popularized in the *Spectator* this use of the word, when writing of 'fairies, witches, magicians, demons, and departed spirits' (in which 'fairy way of writing' Shakespeare 'has incomparably excelled all others'), he says, 'we are led as it were into a new creation,' and 'cannot forbear thinking them natural, though we have no rule by which to judge of them.'[55] In speaking of the power of affecting the imagination, which 'is the very life and highest perfection of poetry,' he says, in a phrase which became famous: 'It has something in it like creation. It bestows a kind of existence, and draws up to the reader's view several objects which are not to be found in being.'[56] Shaftesbury, in his *Characteristicks* (1711), joins together the notion of originality and creation, when he somewhat ironically compares the new and free way of writing with the manufacture of silks and stuffs; each new pattern he says, must be 'an original', and the designer must 'work *originally*, and in a manner *create* each time anew'.[57]

Originality thus acquired a new signification; it came to mean, in the critical parlance of the time, not only the direct observation of Nature, but also the invention or creation of things (for the most part supernatural beings)[58] which did not exist in Nature. This notion of 'creation', and of the artist as a 'creator', soon became current, and before long it began to beget a group of other terms which were needed for its adequate expression. Among these we may note the important adjective *creative*, which, first appearing in the seventeenth century,[59] became, towards the end of the third decade of the eighteenth century, a common adjective in literary criticism. We find it usually in connection with the words 'imagination' or 'fancy', for it was to the imagination that this power of creation was ascribed. David Mallet begins his *Excursion* (1728) with the invocation:

> Companion of the Muse, Creative Power,
> Imagination!

Thomson in his *Summer* writes of Shakespeare's 'creative fancy', and Joseph Warton of his 'lively creative imagination', and calls the *Tempest* 'the most striking instance of his creative power. He has thus given the reins to his boundless imagination, and has carried the romantic, the wonderful, the wild to the most pleasing extravagance.'[60] Thomas Warton, in his *History of Poetry*, speaks of 'the romantic and creative genius of the Arabs',[61] and in Duff's *Essay on Original Genius* (1767) we come on a phrase which has a very modern sound, when he calls 'creative Imagination the distinguishing characteristic of true Genius.'[62]

In phrases such as the above we can see to what extent the imagination has been reinstated as the faculty to which poetry was addressed, and by which it was produced. But if poetry was the product of the imagination; if the imagination was 'creative', and 'originality' was the mark of its 'creations', then a word was needed to describe this special kind of poetic imagination, and the poet who possessed it. Fortunately for the critics of the time there was a word already current which was found capable of absorbing into itself these new conceptions. This was the word *Genius*, the last of the four terms which form the subject of my essay.

IV

To recount in detail the history of the portentous word *Genius* would exhaust my own patience, and still more that of my readers;[63] the briefest summary must suffice for us here. In classical Latin the word *Genius* meant primarily a person's tutelary god or attendant spirit;

and this meaning still survives in our phrase, some one's 'good or evil genius'. It was also used, but rarely in Latin, as more or less a synonym for *ingenium*, 'natural bent and disposition'. In this latter sense the word frequently appears in English in the seventeenth century, meaning both the endowment of natural ability or capacity, and also, occasionally, the person so endowed. Dr Johnson (who in his *Dictionary* did not recognize our modern use of the word) defined the 'true Genius' as a 'mind of large general powers, accidentally determined to some particular direction.'[64] But long before Dr Johnson's time the word had begun to acquire other meanings and associations. The first of these (inherited from the Latin *ingenium*) was that of those special endowments and abilities which fitted a person for some special task. 'A Poet,' Sidney wrote in his *Apology for Poetry*, 'no industrie can make, if his owne *Genius* bee not carried unto it';[65] and Dryden's phrase, 'a happy genius is the gift of nature,' is well known.[66] The word in these uses is equivalent to *talent*, and Dryden uses the two words as synonymous when he says that the description of 'humours' was the particular 'genius and talent' of Ben Jonson.[67] The word came to be tinged also with religious associations, for *Genius* was the name of a god or spiritual being; and later on in the eighteenth century it was used to translate the Arabic word *Jinn*, the good or evil spirits of Arabian mythology. Before, however, this infusion of oriental mystery, the word came to be connected with the ancient term *inspiration*, which, with its half-evaporated classical and religious associations, lingered on in the poetical vocabulary, with the meaning, as Dr Johnson gave it, of 'infusion into the mind by a superior power'. This notion of inspiration, of enthusiasm or daemonic possession, of the 'divine madness' of the poet, is a bit of almost prehistoric psychology, which, embedded in Greek poetry, elaborated and echoed by Aristotle, had bequeathed to the critics of the Renaissance a set of phrases and ideas quite inconsistent with their theory that art was a product of reason, and a copying of Nature. Nor did they attempt to reconcile the two; but the rationalists of the seventeenth and eighteenth centuries, to whom such words as *enthusiasm* and *inspiration* were, from their use by religious fanatics, especially repugnant, became more conscious of this difficulty, which they tried to solve by dismissing the notions these words expressed as impostures or delusions. Hobbes called the invocation of the Muses the reasonless imitation of a foolish custom, 'by which a man, enabled to speak wisely from the principles of Nature and his own meditation, loves rather to be thought to speak by inspiration, like a Bagpipe.'[68] Sir William Davenant declared that the word inspiration was a 'dangerous word', inherited from the dominion-loving poets of the pagan times, who were also priests, and who acquired reverence for themselves by their pretence to inspiration;[69] and Dryden, after saying of Aeschylus that he was 'always in a rapture, . . . the inspiration was still upon him, he was ever tearing it upon the tripos,' goes on to confute those who would justify the madness of poetry from the authority of Aristotle, by suggesting that the text was corrupt; Aristotle had not written that poetry had always something in it either of a man of happy endowments or of a madman; the passage should read 'that it belongs to a witty man, but not to a madman.'[70]

'Every Ass that's Romantick believes he's inspired,' a seventeenth-century critic wrote;[71] and the notion that the pretence to inspiration was either a delusion, or more probably an imposture of poets, devised to give worth to their poetry in vulgar minds, recurs not infrequently in the criticism of the time. But no ridicule could banish this idea of inspiration, based as it was on real experience; for poets, finding that their ideas came to them in special moments of excitement, and from some source as it were outside themselves, would by a natural symbolism still call the poetic impulse a gift from the gods.

The conception, moreover, of a person's genius as his natural bent or disposition, would naturally lead to the notion of this prompting or guiding genius being itself a kind of inspiration; and as early as 1634 we find Sir William Alexander declaring his opinion 'That every Author hath his own Genius, directing him by a secret Inspiration to that wherein he may most excel.'[72] This inborn and, as it were, inspired element in the conception of genius was emphasized by the distinction which was early drawn in English criticism between two kinds of writers, the writers whose talent or genius was the product of study and imitation, and those who were indebted to their natural endowments alone. This distinction, which had been inherited from classical times, and had become a commonplace of Renaissance criticism, was much elaborated in England, and often dwelt on with reference to Shakespeare. It was in fact the tremendous achievement of Shakespeare, his 'originality', his miraculous power of 'creating' supernatural beings, as well as his unprecedented and untutored genius, as they conceived it, which did more than anything else to disintegrate the neo-classical theory of poetry, and replace it by the notions that are expressed in the terms which are the subject of this chapter. For Shakespeare, who 'wanted Art' as Ben Jonson put it, who was, in Milton's phrase, 'Fancy's child', and whose strains were 'native woodnotes wild', came more and more to be regarded as the great example of the 'natural' genius, who by the power of his inborn gifts alone, quite unassisted by art or learning, reached the most sublime levels of artistic achievement. 'The Poetry of Shakespeare was Inspiration indeed,' as Pope expressed it in his famous preface; and although some critics regretted his ignorance ('what would he not have been if he had had learning!'),[73] there were others, even in the seventeenth century, who, like Sir William Temple, suggested that learning might perhaps weaken invention, and lessen the force and growth of genius.[74] Addison, indeed, who had proclaimed Shakespeare as a 'natural' genius, did not claim for him any superiority on this account; but others were more bold, and by the middle of the eighteenth century the glorification of unlearned genius had reached such a point that Dr Johnson felt constrained to denounce the tendency to rely upon it as 'the mental disease of the present generation,'[75] and Sir Joshua Reynolds's *Discourses* were written for the purpose of warning art students against what he called 'the phantom of Inspiration', the false opinion, 'too prevalent among artists, of the imaginary powers of native genius, and its sufficiency in great works.'[76]

We have thus seen how the notions of Originality, and those of Creation and Inspiration, with the ancient and august religious associations of these terms, contributed to deepen the word *genius* with mysterious significations, although we still find it used at the same time – and often by the same writers – with its older and more commonplace meaning, as when we read of a 'polite', an 'ordinary', a 'plodding', and even a 'low and grovelling genius'.

In the twenty-five years which followed the middle of the eighteenth century, a number of *Essays, Reflections,* and *Dissertations* were published, in which the problems connected with Shakespeare, with

Originality, and Genius were discussed.[77] Most of these volumes have been long forgotten; to the lexicographer they are still of interest, but to others their perusal would be indeed a penitential task, for of all the dusty Saharas and Dead Seas of literature, there are none, save perhaps those of old theology, which are more desolate than the arid wastes of obsolete aesthetic speculation.

But these old essays and speculations had their date of eager interest; they represent, no doubt, an immense amount of thinking under the large wigs of that period, and echo a great deal of enthusiastic eighteenth-century discussion. And among them there is one little book which has become famous abroad, and is still dimly remembered in England, where it has been reprinted in recent years. This is the *Conjectures on Original Composition*, published anonymously in 1759, but written by Edward Young, the author of the famous *Night Thoughts*, then in his seventy-seventh year. The book was mainly written, he tells his readers, with the purpose of preserving and giving publicity to an anecdote about Addison; how, when he was on his death-bed, he summoned his stepson in order that he might 'see in what peace a Christian can die'; and there is much pious writing, such as we might expect from an elderly clergyman, in the little volume. But somewhat incongruously infused into this old bottle we find much of the new and intoxicating wine of the Romantic Movement, the glorification of Genius, the praise of originality, the scorn of imitation, and of obedience to the old rules of classical composition, and a buoyant and almost boyish belief in progress, in the future possibilities of great achievement for the emancipated spirit of mankind. The best way, however, to give an impression of these aspects of Young's *Conjectures* will be to quote some of the sentences which are found in it, and which, as we shall see, exploded almost like bombs abroad:

> *Imitations* are of two kinds; one of Nature, one of Authors: The first we call *Originals*, and confine the term *Imitation* to the second. (p. 9.)

> An *Original*, tho' but indifferent (its *Originality* being set aside), yet has something to boast. (p. 11.)

> An *Original* may be said to be of a *vegetable* nature; it rises

spontaneously from the vital root of Genius; it *grows*, it is not made: *Imitations* are often a sort of *Manufacture* wrought up by those *Mechanics, Art,* and *Labour*, out of pre-existent materials not their own. (p. 12.)

Originals can arise from Genius only. (p. 34.)

What, for the most part, mean we by Genius, but the Power of accomplishing great things without the means generally reputed necessary to that end? A *Genius* differs from a *good Understanding*, as a Magician from a good Architect; *That* raises his structure by means invisible; *This* by the skilful use of common tools. Hence Genius has ever been supposed to partake of something Divine. (pp. 26–7.)

Sacer nobis inest Deus, says Seneca. With regard to the Moral world, *Conscience*, and with regard to the Intellectual, *Genius*, is that God within. (pp. 30–1.)

In the Fairyland of Fancy, Genius may wander wild; there it has creative power, and may reign arbitrarily over its own empire of Chimeras. (p. 37.)

So boundless are the bold excursions of the human mind, that in the vast void beyond real existence, it can call forth shadowy beings, and unknown worlds, as numerous, as bright, and, perhaps, as lasting, as the stars; such quite-original beauties we may call Paradisaical, *Natos sine semine flores*, Ovid. (p. 70.)

Many a Genius, probably, there has been, which could neither write, nor read. (p. 35.)

Learning we thank, Genius we revere; That gives us pleasure, This gives us rapture; That informs, This inspires; and is itself inspired. (p. 36.)

To the neglect of Learning, Genius sometimes owes its greater Glory. (p. 29.)

Genius is from Heaven, Learning from man. (p. 36.)

A Star of the first magnitude among the Moderns was

Shakespeare; among the Ancients, *Pindar*; who (as Vossius tells us) boasted of his No-learning, calling himself the Eagle, for his Flight above it. (p. 30.)

An Adult Genius comes out of Nature's hand, as *Pallas* out of *Jove's* head, at full growth, and mature: Shakespeare's Genius was this kind. (p. 31.)

Shakespeare mingled no water with his wine, lower'd his Genius by no vapid Imitation. (p. 78.)

Who knows if *Shakespeare* might not have thought less, if he had read more? (p. 81.)

Born *Originals*, how comes it to pass that we die *Copies*? (p. 42.)

The less we copy the renowned Antients, we shall resemble them the more. (p. 21.)

Let us build our Compositions with the Spirit, and in the Taste, of the Antients; but not with their Materials.[78] (p. 22.)

Phrases with meanings similar to these, if not so pointedly expressed, might be collected from the other treatises I have mentioned; but Young's little book has a much greater importance in the history of culture owing to the fact that it was almost immediately translated into German, where it created, as Herder wrote, an 'electrical' effect, and kindled a blaze of fire in German hearts.

Already, before this date, the ideas of the new criticism had begun to spread in Germany, through the influence of translations from English, and especially, through the writings of the German-Swiss critic Bodmer, who had translated Addison's *Essays on Milton*, and made famous his phrase about the imagination, 'It has something in it like creation.' This idea of the 'creative imagination', suggested but not elaborated by Addison, had become familiar in Germany, and the word *creative*, translated by *schöpferisch*, had aroused the indignation of the pious, one of them describing it as a punishable and blasphemous expression, since the attribute of creation belonged alone to God, and should not be attributed to his creatures.[79]

But in 1760, when Young's book was translated, the time was ripe for a wider and more enthusiastic reception of this new doctrine. The new generation of Germans were eager to free themselves from the tyranny of French classicism; and in the book of Young, and the notions he promulgated, they found the faith, the gospel, and the watchwords which they needed. Young boldly proclaimed the superiority of the original genius, who went direct to Nature, who performed great things by the force of his own inborn powers, untaught by rules and precedents and models; and he declared that Shakespeare was the great original genius of modern times.

In England the popular conception of Shakespeare as a wild, irregular, untutored genius was generally stated apologetically; he had, it was admitted, great faults, but these were condoned by his great and original merits. Above all things he was regarded as inimitable; but Young, on the contrary, declared that he must be imitated; writers should try to be original like Shakespeare, should imitate, not his works, but his methods; they should, like him, disregard all rules and traditions, and go direct to Nature.

It was on this conception of Shakespeare and Shakespeare's methods, and on Young's belief that they could and should be imitated, that the Germans seized with propagandist zeal. The duty of every artist to rely upon his own gifts and inspiration became the fashionable doctrine; and in that wild period, which was called at the time the *Genieperiode*, but has since acquired the name of *Sturm und Drang*, the great watchwords *Genius, Originality*, and *Creative* acquired a resonance, an aggressive and propagandist momentum, which they had certainly never possessed in England.[80] And these terms acquired moreover in Germany a much greater profundity of philosophical meaning, and became the foundation-stones of a metaphysical aesthetic; when we read in Kant that 'creative imagination is the true source of genius and the basis of originality'; that Genius makes rules instead of receiving them; that it embodies in art aesthetic ideas which are creations of the imagination, and suggest more than can be exhausted by any definite concept, we become aware that our home-bred English words have indeed undergone a strange sea-change by being so deeply immersed in the vast and bottomless ocean of Teutonic thought.

What we now call the English Romantic Movement of the eighteenth century hardly deserves indeed, as Professor Beers has pointed out, to be called a movement, since it had 'no leader, no programme, no organ, no theory of art, and very little coherence.'[81] The dilettante bachelors and Church of England clergymen, Gray and Horace Walpole, the Rev. Edward Young, the Rev. Thomas[82] and the Rev. Joseph Warton, Bishop Hurd, and Bishop Percy, were most of them hardly 'Romanticists' at all, but rather amateurs of novelties which amused them; and although in the course of their mild speculations they may have written – and indeed did write – some of these very phrases, they had attached no metaphysical meanings of dark profundity to their casual expressions.

When we now use the word *genius*, the contrasted term *talent* comes into our minds, but this differentiation and contrast, like that of *romantic* and *classical*, is the product of German – or perhaps of French – and not of English cogitation. The *Oxford Dictionary* says:

> It was by German writers of the eighteenth century that the distinction between 'genius' and 'talent,' which had some foundation in French usage,[83] was sharpened into the strong antithesis which is now universally current, so that the one term is hardly ever defined without reference to the other.

Like the antithesis of romanticism and classicism, that between *genius* and *talent* was suggested now and then by English writers, without, however, any emphasis being laid upon it, or any clear distinction drawn; and the word *genius*, with its pagan, and *talent*, with its biblical suggestions, were practically synonymous until the words came back again from Germany. But, as the *Oxford Dictionary* points out, 'when "genius", as native endowment, came to be contrasted with the aptitudes that can be acquired by study, the approach to the modern sense was often very close.'

This distinction indeed grew naturally, and indeed inevitably, out of the conceptions of originality and creation which we have been studying. Genius was, as Kant defined it, *Originalgeist*, Originality was its special mark, it was a Creative Talent. The difference was a difference, not of degree, but of kind; Talent could be acquired; it achieved its effects by imitation and the obedience to rules; Genius was a gift; it was of a nature which obeyed no laws, was a law to itself, and could not be acquired.[84]

The fire which was kindled in German hearts by these watchwords, and the revolutionary ideas they embodied, flamed up in Germany again at the end of the eighteenth century, when a new revolt blazed out in that literary movement which adopted the word *Romantisch* as its battle-cry and title. This title, and the doctrines and propaganda it stood for, was, as we have seen, brought from her German visit by Madame de Staël to set literary France ablaze; and thus the word *romantique*, first borrowed as an epithet for landscape, became in France a literary term to describe those emancipated and revolutionary French writers whom Littré describes.

First from Germany, and then later from France, the echoes and influence of the German and French Romantic Movements began to cross the Channel, bringing with them as their great watchword the English vocable whose adventures and transformations abroad I have briefly recounted. The deeper meanings which had been added to the word *romantic* by German thinkers, and by the opposition they had elaborated between *romanticism* and *classicism*, were made current in England by the writings of Madame de Staël, and also no doubt by the talk of that inexhaustible conversationalist when she came to these shores in 1813.[85]

But before the date of Madame de Staël's English visit we find Jeffrey writing in the *Edinburgh Review* in 1802 of that sect of poets 'who boast much of their originality, and seem to value themselves very highly for having broken loose from the bondage of antient authority, and reasserted the independence of genius.' Though this sect, which had been established in England, Jeffrey said, for ten or twelve years, laid claim to a creed and a revelation of its own, there could be little doubt that their doctrines were 'of German origin, and had been derived from some of the great modern reformers of that country.'[86]

This sect of poets was the School which afterwards was baptized, apparently by Jeffrey, as the 'Lake School',[87] and which in quite recent years we have come to group along with Scott, Byron, Shelley, and Keats as the Romantic Poets of the early nineteenth century.[88] It was to these poets, especially to Coleridge, that we owe our modern familiarity with the great watchwords of modern criticism as we now use, or misuse, them, *originality*, *creative*, *imagination*, and *genius*, as contrasted with *talent*,[89] etc., and from Coleridge the terms were borrowed by Jeffrey and Hazlitt and the other critics of the time.

In more recent times the meanings of all these terms have been much enriched by the modern conception of the unconscious self. Although many psychologists would not now accept, without considerable qualifications, the earlier notion of the Unconscious as the abiding-place of genius, and the source of inspiration, yet they would probably all agree that something analogous to the conscious processes of thought, which may go on beneath awareness, and reveal itself to it in a sudden uprush, probably plays an important, and possibly a dominant, role in what we call inspiration and the creative activity of genius. Although the exact nature of these processes is still a matter of dispute, yet the notion of subconscious thought, taken simply as an unexplained fact of experience, has helped in some degree to make more definite the meanings of the terms we have been discussing.[90] These meanings have been moreover enriched in another way – by the addition, namely, to aesthetic theory, and the facts it considers, of the non-representative arts of architecture and especially of music. It is curious to note, in the bewigged speculations of the eighteenth century, that music, which was the most living art of that time, and especially so in the German home of aesthetic speculation, is barely so much as mentioned. The slightest consideration of the form and content of music would have most effectually shattered the 'imitation-of-nature' theory against which the Germans were in revolt; but in their search for something which transcended Nature, they turned, not to the musical creations of Mozart and Gluck and the other composers of the time, but to the supernatural world which they found in the writings of Shakespeare and Milton and Dante. When precisely the phenomena of music began to exert an influence on German aesthetic theory, I am not learned enough to say,[91] but certainly in English criticism of the time music was only referred to in the briefest and most casual manner.[92]

V

My task has been so far merely the task of the archaeologist of words: I have simply attempted to trace the origins and transformations of a few of our commonest and most hackneyed terms of criticism. But one cannot go on repeating these old battle-cries in cold blood and with complete impunity: the fire still latent in them is contagious; they are ancestral voices which still prophesy of war. Since the aesthetic conflict is by no means ended, and its important issues are a long way from being yet decided, upon the lexicographer also descends the divine fury; the temptation to take up the cudgels and rush, if but for a moment, into the never-ending combat, requires more self-control than I at least can boast of. I must be allowed, therefore, to qualify my narrative with a certain liberty of criticism and comment; and as a preliminary step to joining the speculative war-dance, I shall take this opportunity to point out again how much the origins and adventures of the words we use influence their meaning, and how rich they are in overtones of half-conscious suggestion which confuse us, and which we can only half-comprehend, unless we know their history. That our word *romantic*, for instance, acquired its literary meaning, first of all from the contemptuous attitude of the Age of Reason towards the old romances, and afterwards from its use as an adjective for landscape, for wild and desolate views and ancient castles, seen through the medium of old poems and romances, helps us to understand why, when it was used anew as the name for a certain kind of literature, it came to imply the contemplation of Nature, not directly, but through a mist of associated ideas and literary memories, and thus suggested, and indeed still suggests, that element of subjectivity, of vague and reminiscential feeling, which has been generally regarded as a characteristic of romantic, as opposed to classical, literature. The foreign adventures, too, of the words we have been studying, the fact that they have been to the wars, and have become, as I have said, battle-cries in foreign countries, have also loaded them with propagandist doctrine, with revolutionary and explosive meanings, which are still potent in them. This is especially true, I think, of the great watchwords *Genius* and *Originality*; the *Genieperiode* in Germany, the Romantic Movements, both in Germany and France, were times of angry enthusiasm and of wild revolt; the ecstatic emphasis laid upon the freedom, the spontaneity, and the originality of the creative genius, the attribution to that genius of miraculous and daemonic powers, invested the cult of Genius and the worship of Originality with an exaggerated and mystical importance. The artists of earlier days had been regarded – and had regarded themselves – as craftsmen; the new conception of the artist as a genius, as a creature of passion and fire, above the law, and the popular deification of this ideal, tended to produce the beings thus imagined and adored – the wild spirits of lawless lives and strange fits of passion,

And mighty Poets in their misery dead.

The emphasis, too, on originality, on the expression of the artist's unique personality, on the never-ceasing creation of something new and strange and never before heard of, has not only tended to inflame the vanity of the artist, but also to suggest standards of comparison and valuation in which the elements of novelty, of newness for its own sake, are somewhat unduly overprized. The work of a great artist always, or almost always, has in it an element of newness, and is always, or almost always (though without conscious purpose), coloured by his own personality. But these are surely more accidental than essential characteristics of his work; for newness and the expression of unique personalities are of no great artistic importance in themselves. This is especially true in the arts which we call the fine arts, where technique and tradition are of prime importance; and it would not perhaps be too fantastic to attribute, in part at least, the downfall of painting, architecture, and the handicrafts in the earlier decades of the nineteenth century – perhaps the greatest artistic disaster the world has ever suffered – to this modern enthusiasm for the originality of creative genius, and the desire on the part of every artist and architect and handicraftsman to display as conspicuously as possible his own personality and peculiar gifts. Ever since then the history of art has been the history of conscious and violent revolutions and reactions, instead of that gradual and unconscious modification of an inherited tradition which characterized its development in previous ages.

How far the antithesis, developed abroad, in our conceptions of classical and romantic art has been an advantage or disadvantage to criticism it would be difficult to say; but most of us would agree, I think, that this antithesis has been greatly over-emphasized. The words *romanticism* and *classicism* are used like hatchets to chop us materials of the most delicate and subtle weaving and intertexture; and indeed the variety of meaning attributed to them shows that they are employed without any precise and accepted understanding of what their signification really is. For what after all is romanticism as contrasted with classicism? Is it, as Pater said, the addition of strangeness to beauty; is it disease as opposed to health, as Goethe defined it; or an appeal to the feelings as against an appeal to reason; or as Schlegel said, the picturesque contrasted with the statuesque; or self-abandonment versus self-control; individualism as opposed to the ideals of organized society; associated ideas and subjectivity as contrasted with objectivity and formal beauty; the exotic, the bizarre, and the magical and mysterious moment, rather than the typical, the usual, the general? Or shall we define it as suggestiveness, incompleteness, aspiration, and a preoccupation with the infinite, as opposed to definiteness, completeness, and precision of statement?

It is perhaps all these things; but if this is so, there are both romantic and classical elements in almost every work of art; and the exaggerated opposition between the two makes it necessary to distort the facts, if we are to place poems and plays and pictures each separately by itself in one or the other of these categories. The facts are really too complex to be summed up in any one formula; and indeed, all the terms we have been discussing tend to distort and caricature the phenomena they attempt to account for; it would have been better, perhaps, for English criticism if they had remained at home, and by half-conscious adjustments, adapted themselves, in the practical, empirical, muddle-headed English way, to the new facts of aesthetic appreciation as they spontaneously arose. However, we must take them as they come to our hands; if they are ploughshares which have been beaten into swords, tools which have been made into battle-axes, they are tools nevertheless for which we have no substitutes, and we cannot, if we wish to write of the aesthetic problems which face us do without them. These problems are of two kinds: there are those connected with the work of art itself, and those which are more intimately concerned with the artist who produces it. In every representative of Nature which is a work of art, there is to be found, as Prof. Courthope has said, something which is not to be found in the aspect of Nature which it represents; and what that something is has been a matter of dispute from the earliest days of criticism. This is the aspect of the problem which has most interested the neo-classical critics; those of what we call romantic tendencies have paid more attention to its subjective aspect,[93] the power of faculty in the artist which has enabled him to add this unknown something to his representation of Nature. What is it, they have asked, which differentiates the artistic imagination from the mere fancy, or from the imagination which produces dreams or the illusions of illness or of madness? If we call it the 'plastic' or the 'creative' imagination, we can then perhaps call its product a 'creation', rather than a 'finding' or 'invention'; and the power of the creative artist we many designate as genius, as opposed to talent. Thus the artist himself becomes a genius, and we are fitted out with a makeshift vocabulary of terms for our critical discriminations. But these terms are, as we have seen, the product of much confused and over-excited thinking; and they denote rather than they define and explain the phenomena they describe. If, however, we are unable to use them scientifically, a knowledge of their history may perhaps, as I have suggested, help to put us on our guard against them when they patently distort the facts. If we keep in mind the revolutionary origin of our modern theory of genius, we may discount some of the more overwhelming reverberations of this portentous word, and more clearly perceive the element of truth which it certainly does express. Now there can be no doubt that the spontaneous, inspired daemonic genius – or at least, since it is more a matter of degree than of absolute distinction – that the genius who possesses more conspicuously than others this character, has existed in all the arts: El Greco in painting, Michael Angelo in sculpture, Wagner in music, are analogues of original poets like Shelley, Blake, or Walt Whitman; but the emphasis laid upon the type of genius possessed by these great originators, and the depreciatory contrast with mere talent, has tended, I think, to make us forget that the daemonic genius is not the only kind of genius, and indeed not by any means always the greatest kind.

We tend to relegate the undaemonic artists to the category of talent;

and if the antithesis between genius and talent is, as no doubt it is, a useful one, it might be well to restore to our vocabulary the other and older antithesis between the 'natural' and the 'learned' genius. For there are poets and artists of the first rank who are endowed with no daemonic qualities. If Aeschylus was, as Dryden said, a great genius, and always 'tearing it upon the tripos', we cannot deny the appellation of genius to Sophocles, who indulged in no such contortions. So in every age of art we find the same contrast. It would be absurd to refuse the name of genius to Milton or to Leopardi, and yet there were never more conscious authors; and, to take another instance, Charlotte Brontë is regarded by her admirers as a more inspired genius than Jane Austen, but would they maintain that she is therefore a greater writer? Is the inspired Blake a more important figure in English art than the laborious, learned, conscientious Sir Joshua Reynolds? One of the great defects of our critical vocabulary is the lack of a neutral, non-derogatory name for these great artificers, these artists who derive their inspiration more from the formal than the emotional aspects of their art, and who are more interested in the masterly control of their material, than in the expression of their own feelings, or the prophetic aspects of their calling.

For this kind of genius, and for the quality which distinguishes it, I should like to suggest an adjective and a noun which will at first certainly surprise, and perhaps shock, my readers, but which, both from their etymology and their earlier use, fit most exquisitely the meaning for which we so much need them. These are the words *erudite* and *erudition*, which are derived from *erudire* (*e*, 'out of', and *rudis*, 'rude', 'rough', or 'raw'), a verb meaning in classical Latin to bring out of the rough, to form by means of art, to polish, to instruct. *Eruditus* has in Latin the meaning of 'accomplished', 'skilled'; and in its earlier English use it kept its classical meaning. So also *erudition* was used for the process of training or instruction, 'the erudition of young children'; and also for the instruction thus imparted, and for the state of being trained or instructed; and it was thus used by Shakespeare.[94] It was also used of the perfect workmanship or finish of a coin, Addison for instance writing that 'the intrinsic value of an old coin does not consist in its metal but its erudition.'[95]

If, then, we could restore *erudite* and *erudition* to their old meanings (they are now merely superfluous synonyms for 'learned' and 'learning'), we should have fitting appellations for our great artificers, and for that quality of conscious artistry, of acquired technical accomplishment, which cannot, when carried, as by Horace, to exquisite perfection, be called mere talent. A name for this noble kind of genius, which would explicate and make clear and emphasize its nature and its methods, would I think be of special advantage in two ways. It would, in the first place, recall attention to the imitable qualities in high artistic achievement; for the erudite genius, with his acquired mastery of his material, can be most profitably imitated; while, as Sir Joshua Reynolds pointed out, the imitation of the daemonic genius and his reliance on his inborn and untutored powers, is (save for other daemonic geniuses like himself) the worst possible precedent and example. Then also the fact that the daemonic genius is often a prophet as well, and is generally thought to have a mission (though what exactly were Shakespeare's or Keats's missions it might be difficult to say), has given rise to the notion that the true genius comes, like Wordsworth or Shelley or Browning or Walt Whitman, with a message for his age; and thus the genius who has no gospel, no scheme of salvation for the world, but simply a genius for pure art, suffers disparagement from others, and perhaps discouragement in himself.

It would perhaps be better for our criticism if we were to use the word *genius* to describe the gift and endowment, rather than the person thus gifted and endowed; or even, as a critic has suggested,[96] for us to avoid using the term as far as possible, and to rehabilitate and restore the term *inspiration*. For inspiration, and the notion it suggests, is perhaps a better description than genius for the phenomena of artistic achievement. The word genius implies the permanent possession of magical power; and all the works of a genius, being regarded as the products of this power, are accepted in a spirit of worship and without discrimination. Thus criticism is blurred, and the genius himself, believing in the unfailing potency of his gift, tends to work in a slovenly manner, and is tempted also to exaggerate and exploit the wonder-working personality to which are attributed such miraculous results. But artists even of the greatest genius are, as we all know, quite capable of producing work of the most deplorable and unblest description; their genius is at best but an intermittent energy, and the greatest artist or poet is simply the artist or poet who is most subject to the visitation of what we call inspiration – who is more frequently and more powerfully inspired than other men. Shelley, who was perhaps as richly endowed with what we call genius as any poet who ever existed, has well described the coming and going of the inspiration upon which, as he tells us, the poet must depend.

> Poetry is not like reasoning, a power to be exerted according to the determination of the will. A man cannot say, 'I will compose Poetry.' The greatest poet even cannot say it; for the mind in creation is as a fading coal, which some invisible influence, like an inconstant wind, awakens to transitory brightness; this power arises from within, like the colour of a flower which fades and changes as it is developed, and the conscious portions of our natures are unprophetic either of its approach or its departure.[97]

In the intervals of inspiration, the poet, Shelley adds, 'becomes a man, and is abandoned to the sudden reflux of the influences under which others habitually live.'

If our attention were more habitually directed to the visits of inspiration, rather than to the genius it visits, although a clear conception of what inspiration is might elude us, yet we could more accurately discriminate its traces, finding them not only in the works of the erudite as well as the daemonic genius, but also, now and then, in the productions of mere men of talent, to whom the name of genius, with its modern meaning, can hardly be applied.

The advance of modern psychology has, moreover, removed one difficulty which to the older critics was involved in the theory of inspiration. If poetry, they asked, was a product of inspiration, if it was something which was given from without how could it be regarded as an art which required – as poetry obviously did require – labour, apprenticeship, preparation, study? This difficulty is met for us by the modern theory of the unconscious, and all the real, if loosely defined, notions which are associated with that concept.[98] Inspiration, as we conceive it, does not come to us from without. It is not a gift of the stars or the Muses, but an impulse from sources that are inside ourselves. The Pierian Spring, the Fountain of Castalia, are still flowing, but their streams murmur deep within us; and although our conscious intelligence has no direct control over these springs of power, yet by labour and study it can clarify and enrich them; and can form standards and ideals which, long brooded over, may then sink down from the conscious into the unconscious strata of our mental existence, and mould and elaborate the unknown stores of energy which exist there, amorphous and concealed.

The modern cult of Genius, and the heated atmosphere of revolution that gave it birth, have also tended to over-emphasize and endow with exaggerated importance the word *originality*, and the quality it denotes in works of art. Originality has no doubt its importance, but that importance is more historical than purely aesthetic; for not only in the absence of documents are we unable to say how much originality is possessed by the works of ancient writers like Homer or Lucretius or Catullus,[99] but also, when we do possess the documents, we often find that the greatest innovators in the arts, those who have done most to create new forms and utilize new material, are not by any means always those of the highest and most permanent achievement. Donne was a greater innovator than Shakespeare, and had a much more powerful influence upon the succeeding generation, but he was not a greater poet; Caravaggio was one of the most original of Italian painters, and has been called the first modern artist, the inventor of realism, the begetter of Velasquez and Manet; but his work has for us little pure artistic interest. Rossetti was a painter of immense originality, but of small artistic achievement; Philipp Emanuel Bach, musicians tell us, was a greater originator, and had a much more powerful influence on the development of music, than his father John Sebastian; while Jean-Jacques Rousseau is by no means the greatest writer of that world of modern thought and feeling which he did more than any one to discover and create. The sense of original discovery, of turning up new soil, is more of value as an incentive and encouragement to the artist, than as an approved ingredient in, or characteristic of, his work.

Besides the word *inspiration*, there is another rather old-fashioned term which we might do well to furbish up and restore to our critical vocabulary. This is the painter's term *invention*, which describes a quality of real, if subordinate, importance, not only in painting but in literature as well. Johnson declared that the highest praise of poetry was invention, 'such invention as, by producing something unexpected, surprises and delights.'[100] It was by invention, he said, that 'new trains of events are formed, and new scenes of imagery displayed';[101] and this power not only of inventing new scenes and incidents and displaying new images, but also of contriving new moulds and shapes, metrical and other, for the purposes of new expression – this gift of invention, which Keats called 'the Polar Star of Poetry,'[102] has been somewhat overshadowed and eclipsed by the use of the portentous word *creation*, with which I shall conclude my remarks. The words *create, creation, creator, creative*, have become so vulgarized, and are so indiscriminately used – even in fashion-papers we read of 'creations' in millinery – that careful writers try to avoid them, although they find that they cannot banish them altogether from their vocabulary. For the conception they embody is, of all the ideas expressed by the watchwords we have been studying, in fact the primary one; it lies at the root of all the rest, and is the origin and source of the great change in our modern theory of aesthetics. The word *invention* was a word of compromise, an attempt to reconcile, by the idea of original copying, the old imitation-theory with the notorious need for something more than the repetition of the same effects in art. As this imitation-theory gradually broke down, the notion of invention began to be replaced by that of creation – the creation, in the first place, of 'fairy worlds' by Shakespeare and Milton, but especially by Shakespeare. This conception was then enlarged to include the creation in drama and fiction of living characters, and afterwards with the inclusion of music, to that of whole new and spontaneous worlds of feeling and relation, which have little or no correspondence with the given world of fact.

This idea, like the other ideas we have been studying, was immensely emphasized in the romantic revolts of Germany and France: to sanctify and deify art as the second creator was, Theophile Gautier tells us, one of the ideals of the French Romantics, and he quotes the famous lines:

> Dans la création d'un bonheur sans mélange
> Etre plus artiste que Dieu![103]

This reverent and religious, or, as others thought it, irreligious, conception of the divine power of the artistic creator returned across the Channel, and is often found in the works of Coleridge, as when, for instance, he describes the imagination of the artist as an echo of what he calls the primary imagination, which is itself an analogue of creation, and its activity 'a repetition in the finite mind of the eternal act of creation in the infinite I AM.'[104] In other writers of this period, in Wordsworth and Keats and Shelley and Hazlitt, we find an almost equal glorification of the poet's creative faculty, the notion that the artist, and above all the poet, has the power of creating a new heaven and a new earth, a world more real perhaps than the actual one, a universe of the mind, concrete, autonomous, independent, and peopled by living beings, created before they are represented – as Coleridge said of Shakespeare's characters – out of the depths of the poet's own mind, and, in Shelley's words,

> Forms more real than living man,
> Nurslings of immortality.

There is something mystical in this doctrine, this faith, as of Keats, that 'what the Imagination seizes as Beauty must be Truth – whether it existed before or not.' And yet the notion that art is creative, that, in Pater's words, it 'adds a new presence to the world', or as Wordsworth puts it, 'Genius is the introduction of a new element into the intellectual universe . . . an advance, or a conquest, made by the soul of the poet,' is a notion which deeply permeates all our criticism; and what we have come to value most in art is not the imitation of Nature, but the unprecedented and undreamed of harmonies it creates, the surprise and strangeness of those authentic and yet unforeseeable visions – those worlds of beauty and truth and wonder – which it opens to the imagination.

Even in a phrase like:

> Tiger! Tiger! burning bright
> In the forests of the Night,

we seem to recognize the character of something inevitable, something that has a veracity of its own, that must exist, and has always existed, and from which we cannot withhold the name of reality.

And as often happens in the history of thought, our notion of this mystery of artistic creation has been made somewhat clearer by the method of antithesis. Just as romanticism has been more clearly defined by its opposition to classicism, genius by the contrast with talent, and imagination by that of fancy, so the notion of creation has been sometimes contrasted with that of invention, as when for instance a recent critic wrote that 'Shakespeare of all men seems to have been in comparison with his strength in Creation, the weakest in Invention.'[105]

VI

In their human and most happy manner the ancient Greeks embodied in appropriate symbols their awareness of aesthetic facts and of the experience of the poet. These symbols of Apollo, the lyre of the God, and the piercing song of the Muses, their haunts on Helicon and Parnassus, their sacred springs of Hippocrene and Castalia; the visits of these Immortals to the mortals who invoke them, and the divine fury and enthusiasm they inspire, have lived on in our literature, not only as hallowed and beautiful ornaments, but as true, though symbolic, expressions of the circumstances which give rise to poetry, and of the nature of the poet's sensibilities and gifts. To this inherited vocabulary the Romantic Movement has added, partly from biblical sources, the terms which have been occupying our attention. The whole body of these words, ancient and modern, represents and expresses the aesthetic experience of the human spirit; an experience which, though very real and profound, has been as yet very partially clarified into speculative theory. But these words have come to be so indiscriminately employed, and are now so blurred in outline, that there is a great need to make definite, and *préciser* – or why not say in purer English 'to precise' – their meanings; to bring into more clear-cut relief the phenomena they designate; and by means of a nicer and more accurate use of this inherited vocabulary, to discriminate for instance in works of art their originality, their romantic or their classical ingredients; or, in the endowments of the artist who produces them, their gifts of talent and erudition, or of unconscious and daemonic genius. And if, becoming aware of other qualities for which we have no names, we may be tempted to suggest new appellations, we would do well to follow, in this matter, the tradition of our older nomenclature, and be content, for the most part, like our predecessors, with designating or merely descriptive words. There is a tendency in the human mind to be impatient of anything it cannot understand, and to deny, if possible, the existence of phenomena for which it can find no explanation. Thus, as we have seen, the neo-classical critics denied the existence of inspiration, and the more mysterious powers of the imagination. This tendency leads men of science to prefer analytic and explanatory terms; but in matters like the phenomena of aesthetics, names which may suggest over-hasty explanations tend to falsify and distort the things they designate, and become premature and petrified definitions, which cannot readily grow and deepen with the growth and deepening of our knowledge. A chance appellation like *romantic*, for instance, or a metaphor like *inspiration*, are much more convenient names than a term like Coleridge's 'esemplastic power' for the imagination, which attempts to explain its working.

The truth is that the phenomena of artistic production are still so obscure, so baffling, we are still so far from an accurate scientific and psychological knowledge of their genesis or meaning, that we are forced to accept them as empirical facts; and empirical and non-explanatory names are the names that suit them best. The complete explanation of any fact is the very last step in human thought; and it is reached, as I have said, if indeed it is ever reached, by the preliminary processes of recognition, designation, and definition. It is with these preliminary processes that our aesthetic criticism is still occupied. We have recognized, and we have named, the mysterious creative power of the imagination, the genius of the poet or artist who possesses it, and the inspiration by which he is himself possessed. But what, stated in terms of scientific psychology, these powers really are, and what are the conditions which favour or impede their activity, though they are problems whose solution is of the utmost importance for civilization, they are problems nevertheless about which we are still almost completely in the dark. Perhaps the most profitable thing we can do at present is, leaving their ultimate analysis in suspense, to discriminate their manifestations in the immense wealth of concrete examples to which our attention is being now so multifariously directed. The more adequate solution of these problems is a task which will no doubt profoundly concern the critics, the psychologists, and even the sociologists and metaphysicians of the future; it is not, however, a task which can rightly be imposed upon the lexicographer, whose peaceful role I now resume, and in which role I will complete my essay by a few relevant quotations from some of our contemporary writers who have touched upon these problems. Thus Mr A. C. Bradley says of poetry, 'Its nature is to be not a part, not yet a copy, of the real world (as we commonly understand that phrase), but to be a world by itself, independent, complete, autonomous.' And again, of life and poetry, he says, 'the two may be called different forms of the same thing; one of them having (in the usual sense) reality, but seldom fully satisfying imagination; while the other offers something which satisfies imagination, but has not full "reality".'[106]

In writing of Byron, Dr Herford says:

> Byron lacks supreme imagination. With boundless resources of invention, rhetoric, passion, wit, fancy, he has not the quality which creates out of sensation, or thought, or language, or all together, an action, a vision, an image, or a phrase, which, penetrated with the poet's individuality, has the air of a discovery, not an invention, and no sooner exists than it seems to have always existed. A creator in the highest sense Byron is not.'[107]

In the writings of the least romantic of modern critics, Mr Santayana, we can perhaps find the most rational statement of this modern theory of artistic creation.

> A spontaneous creation of the mind can be more striking and living than any reality, or any abstraction from realities. The artist can invent a form which, by its adaptation to the imagination, lodges there, and becomes a point of reference for all observations, and a standard of naturalness and beauty . . . This method of originating types is what we ordinarily describe as artistic

creation. The name indicates the suddenness, originality, and individuality of the conception thus attained.[108]

In another place Mr Santayana says of the higher arts:

When the world is shattered to bits they can come and 'build it nearer to the heart's desire.' The great function of poetry . . . is precisely this: to repair to the material of experience, seizing hold of the reality of sensation and fancy beneath the surface of conventional ideas, and then out of that living but indefinite material to build new structures, richer, finer, fitter to the primary tendencies of our nature, truer to the ultimate possibilities of the soul.'[109]

I will end with a relevant quotation from a living poet:

> For beauty being the best of all we know
> Sums up the unsearchable and secret aims
> Of nature, and on joys whose earthly names
> Were never told can form and sense bestow;
> And man hath sped his instinct to outgo
> The step of science; and against her shames
> Imagination stakes out heavenly claims,
> Building a tower above the head of woe.[110]

1. (See below, note 15). The adjective is found in Evelyn's *Diary* under the date of 1654 (see below, note 25). As, however, Evelyn edited, or re-wrote, his diary towards the end of his life, it cannot be relied upon as a safe indication of linguistic usage. The etymology of the word is well known; 'a whole chapter of literary history is included in the derivation of *Romantic* from Rome; it tells of the rise of rude popular dialects, alongside the learned and polished Latin, in the various provinces of the Roman Empire; and of the rise of modern European fiction, written so distinctively in these dialects that it got its name from them': W. D. Whitney, *Language and the Study of Language* (1867), p. 131.

2. It was borrowed into French and German from English; Grimm's *Wörterbuch*, however, quotes from a Latin MS. of the fifteenth century an instance of *romanticus* used as a term for a fictitious tale (article *Romantisch*). In the Life of Sir Philip Sidney, which was written by Fulke Greville, Lord Brooke, probably before 1612, but which was not published until 1652, occurs the phrase, 'Doe not his Arcadian Romanties live after him?' (p. 13). The word *Romanties* in this passage might perhaps be regarded (and so the Editor of the *Oxford Dictionary* seems to have regarded it) as a misprint for *Romantics*, but in a MS. version of the *Life* in the library of Trinity College, Cambridge, the word is spelt *Romantiae*. In the printed version however the impression of the *e* in *Romanties* is not a clear one and might easily be mistaken for a *c*; and it is not impossible that our word *romantic* owes its origin to a contemporary misreading of this kind. Fulke Greville's *Romanties* may be a variant of the Chaucerian word *Romaunte*.

3. S.P.E. *Tract* III., p. 19.

4. Thomas Shadwell, Preface to the *Sullen Lovers*, 1668. Spingarn, *Critical Essays of the Seventeenth Century*, vol. ii, p. 150. (I shall refer in future to this collection as Spingarn.)

5. *Ibid.* p. 61.

6. *On Ancient and Modern Learning*, 1690, *ibid.* vol. iii. p. 71.

7. The phrase 'romantic love', which has acquired so rich a meaning in modern times, was used somewhat differently in the eighteenth century. A writer in *The World*, for instance (No. 79, July 4, 1754), mentions some ladies who had remained unmarried because their imaginations had been 'early perverted with the Chimerical ideas of Romantic Love', according to which passion, he adds, 'a footman may as well be the hero as his master'; and he tells the story of Clarinda, who, instead of marrying the suitable Theodore, fell in love with his French valet Antoine, there being 'no resisting of the impetuosity of romantic love'.

8. Hurd, *Letters on Chivalry and Romance*, 1762. (Ed. 1911, p. 153.)

9. 'I saw Hamlet Prince of Denmark played, but now the old plays begin to disgust this refined age, since his Majestie's being so long abroad.' (*Diary of John Evelyn*, 26 Nov. 1661), quoted by T. S. Perry, *English Literature in the Eighteenth Century*. It should, however, be noted that the word *disgust* was in former times a milder term than it is now. (See Mr R. W. Chapman's notes on Jane Austen's English, in his edition of *Emma*, 1923, p. 398.)

10. *Observations on the Faerie Queene* (1754), p. 237.

11. *Advancement of Learning*, Book II.

12. *Midsummer-Night's Dream*, v. i. 7–17.

13. Spingarn, vol. ii. p. 58. The introduction to these volumes contains a lucid history of the concept of Imagination in the earlier and later periods of criticism.

14. *Essays of John Dryden* (Ker), vol. i. p. 229.

15. It is perhaps more than a coincidence that in the first instance which has been found of the adjective *romantic*, it is used in close connection with the word imagination. 'As for *Imagination*, there is no question but that Function is mainly exercised in the chief seat of the Soul, those purer Animal Spirits in the fourth Ventricle of the Brain. I speak especially of that Imagination which is most free, such as we use in *Romantick Inventions*.' (H. More, *The Immortality of the Soul*, 1659, p. 228.)

16. *Epistle to Dr. Arbuthnot*, 1735, 340–1.

17. *Spectator*, No. 303 (1712).

18. 'The subject and scene of this tragedy, so romantic and uncommon, are highly pleasing to the imagination.' J. Warton on Pope (1757), ed. 1806, i. p. 71 n.

19. Preface to second edition of *Castle of Otranto*, 1765.

20. *Moral Essays*, Ep. II., 16.

21. *Natural History of Wiltshire* (1847), p. 108.

22. J. Britton, *Memoir of John Aubrey* (1845), pp. 32–3.

23. *Evelyn's Diary*, ed. Bray, vol. ii. p. 81.

24. 26 Feb. 1666.

25. *Evelyn*, vol. ii. p. 54. First noted I believe by T. S. Perry in his *English Literature in the Eighteenth Century*. In another entry of 1654 Evelyn uses the word again: Bray, vol. ii. p. 84.

26. Ibid., vol. ii. pp. 353–4.

27. *Addison's Works*, edited by Richard Hurd, vol. i. p. 359.

28. *Spectator*, No. 74.

29. Quoted in Phelps, *The English Romantic Movement*, Boston, 1902, p. 98.

30. The *Adventurer*, No. 108, 17 Nov. 1753.

31. Shaftesbury's *Moralists* (1709): Works (1732), vol. ii. p. 394.

32. What is said to be the earliest instance of the word *romantique* in French is found in 1675, where it is obviously borrowed from English. In 1666 a M. de Sorbière published a *Relation d'un voyage en Angleterre*; and in 1668 Thomas Sprat wrote an anonymous little book of *Observations* on this book of travel, in which he says (p. 37) of Sorbière, 'He speaks so *Romantically* of the *Vallies*, the *Hills*, and the

hedges of *Kent*, that the *Authors of Clelia*, or *Astrea*, scarce ever venture to say so much on the like occasion.' In 1675 was published at Amsterdam an account of this *Réponse* of Sprat's, in which it is said, 'L'auteur anonyme blâme Sorbière d'avoir parlé *en termes romantiques* des vallées, des montagnes et des haies verdoyantes du pays de Kent' (quoted, *Revue d'Histoire Littéraire de France*, 1911, p. 440).

33. *Annales de la Société Jean-Jacques Rousseau* (Paris), vol. v. (1909). See also further notes by M. François in the *Bibliothèque Universelle et Revue Suisse* (Lausanne), August and September 1918. Senancour added to the thirty-eighth letter of his *Obermann* a fragment (the third fragment) *de l'expression Romantique et du Ranz des Vaches*, in which he attempts to define the distinction between *romantique* and *romanesque*, the one appealing to deep souls and true sensibilities, the other to *les imaginations vives et fleuries*. In the best French usage of to-day the distinction which is made between *romantique* and *romanesque* is, I am informed on good authority, somewhat different. *Romantique* is used with a more or less definite reference to the French Romantic Movement, and the ways of feeling and the tastes of the French 'Romantics'. It has, therefore, a certain historical connotation, and any manifestations of romanticism noted in an earlier epoch would be described as *romantisme avant la lettre*. In our phrases 'romantic love', 'romantic friendship', etc., 'romantic' would be translated by *romanesque*; the use of *romantique* in this connexion generally implying emotions as they were felt and described by the contemporaries of Chateaubriand or Victor Hugo.

34. Written in 1777, first published in 1782.

35. Rousseau made use of this expression before he adopted *romantique* into his vocabulary, when, in his famous description of the mountains of Valais (which passage has been described as 'the first flowering of romantic sentiment in French literature'), he says, 'Enfin, ce spectacle a je ne sais quoi de magique, de surnaturel, qui ravit l'esprit et les sens' (*Nouvelle Héloise*, 1760, i. *Lettre XXIII.*). For the history of the non-descriptive, non-explanatory, and purely identifying term of the French Précieuses, *je ne sais quoi*, see Spingarn, vol. i. p. c. It appears in England as a substantive in the latter part of the seventeenth century; Shaftesbury attempted to define its critical significance, calling it 'the unexpressible, the unintelligible, the *I-know-not-what* of Beauty', 'a kind of *charm* or *enchantment* of which the artist himself can give no account' (*Characteristicks*, 1711, ed. 1731, vol. i. p. 332; vol. ii. p. 413). Another term for romantic landscape was *horrid*, and the plea-

sure it gave was described as 'a pleasing kind of *horror*'. Shaftesbury writes of the 'horrid Graces of the *Wilderness*', etc. (ibid. ii. p. 393).

36. See Grimm's *Wörterbuch*, s. v. *Romantisch*.

37. Thomas Warton, in his *Observations on the Faerie Queene*, (1754), speaks of 'the romantic species of poetical composition introduced by the provençal bards' (p. 1). He describes Spenser as a 'romantic poet' (p. 217), and to his *History of English Poetry* (1774) he prefixes a dissertation entitled 'Of the origin of Romantic Fiction in Europe.'

38. Although never emphasized or worked out as in Germany, the contrast between romantic and classical literature is occasionally alluded to in English criticism of the eighteenth century. Thus in his *Letters on Chivalry* (1762), Hurd says Tasso 'trimmed between the Gothic and the Classic' (p. 114); the Faerie Queen 'is a Gothic, not a classical poem' (p. 115), 'Spenser tried to unite the Gothic, and the Classic unity' (p. 124). Thomas Warton, as Prof. Ker has pointed out, actually uses the words *romantic* and *classical* when, in writing of Dante, he speaks of 'This wonderful compound of classical and romantic fancy' (*History of English Poetry*, vol. iii. 1781, p. 241). Hurd also contrasts the romantic and classic customs or 'manners' (*Letters on Chivalry*, p. 148).

39. Eckermann, *Conversations of Goethe*, March 21, 1830 (English Translation 1850, vol. ii. p. 273).

40. Victor Hugo says, in the preface of 1824 to his *Odes et Ballades*, that it was this *femme de génie* who first pronounced the phrase *littérature romantique* in France.

41. A writer in the *Quarterly Review* of October 1814, speaks of the attempts that had recently been made, especially in Germany, to simplify the old debate about the merits of the Ancients and the Moderns by calling the productions of antiquity *classic*, and those of modern time *romantic*; and adds in a note, 'Madame de Staël has made the British public familiar with these expressions' (quoted *OED*). Byron in his answer to Bowles's criticism of Pope (1821) says that Schlegel and Madame de Staël have endeavoured to reduce poetry to '*two* systems, classical and romantic' (Byron's *Works*, vol. v. p. 554 n.). In a letter written in 1820 he says that these terms had not been in use when he left England (in 1816), (ibid. p. 104).

42. ''Tis with Originall Poems as with Originall Pieces of Painters, whose Copies abate the excessive price of the first Hand,' Sir W. Davenant, *Preface to Gondobert*, 1650 (Spingarn, vol. ii. p. 5).

43. Dryden's *Essays* (Ker), vol. i. p. 228.

44. *Originalité* has been found in French in 1699; the word was admitted in

the Dictionary of the French Academy in 1762. The earliest instance I
have found of the word in English is in a letter of Gray's of 24 May 1742
(*Gray's Letters*, ed. Tovey, vol. i. p. 107). On 14 July of the same year
Horace Walpole wrote to Mann at Florence, about a picture which he
wished Mann to purchase for Sir Robert Walpole; 'It is one of the most
engaging pictures I ever saw. I have no qualms about its originality'
(*Walpole's Letters*, ed. Toynbee, vol. 1. p. 256). The word soon came
into fairly common use among the more romantically inclined critics,
and in 1766 the Shakespearean commentator, E. Capell, published a
book with the title *Reflections on Originality in Authors*.

45. Leonard Welsted, *A Dissertation concerning the State of Poetry* (1724),
printed in Durham's *Critical Essays of the Eighteenth Century* (1895),
p. 377.

46. 'This primary or original *copying*, which in the ideas of Philosophy is
Imitation, is, in the language of Criticism, called INVENTION' (Hurd,
A Discourse on Poetical Imitation). In Hurd's edition of Horace's
Epistolae ad Pisones et Augustum, 1757, vol. ii. p. 106.

47. Dryden's *Essays* (Ker), vol. ii. p. 138.

48. Ker, vol. i. p. 15.

49. Hazlitt, *Collected Works*, vol. xii. p. 367.

50. *Apology for Heroic Poetry and Poetic Licence* (Ker), vol. i. p. 187.

51. *Preface to Troilus and Cressida* (1679), Ker, vol. i. p. 219.

52. Although *creare* is not uncommon in classical Latin, *condere* is the
more usual term. *Creare*, with its derivative *creator* (rare as a classical
term), is very common in ecclesiastic Latin, where it expressed the
non-classical idea of creation out of nothing – that central doctrine of a
special creation out of nothing upon which the Christian theology is
based. *Condere*, like the Greek κτίζειν, implied the making, or the
bringing into being, of something out of pre-existent material. In the
later use of *creare* was explicit the meaning which the English word
inherited, and which Dr Johnson defined, in his *Dictionary*, as 'to form
out of nothing.'

53. The element of 'making' implied in the etymology of 'Poet' was
generally translated by the word 'maker' or 'feigner' by the earlier
English critics, such as Sidney and Webbe; Puttenham, however, says
that if poets could 'make all things out of them selves, without any
subject of veritie, then they be (by maner of speech) as creating gods' (G.
Gregory Smith, *Elizabethan Critical Essays*, vol. ii. p. 4). Puttenham is
no doubt echoing here the famous phrase from Scaliger's *Poetics: velut
alter deus condere* (ibid. i. 386). Donne, in one of his sermons (preached

probably in 1632), says: 'Poetry is a counterfeit Creation, and makes things that are not, as though they were' (*LXXX. Sermons*, 1640, p. 266). Bacon uses the word with reference to discoveries, *Inventa quasi novae creationes sunt et divinorum operum imitamenta* (*Nov. Org.* i. 129). Shakespeare uses it of mental images:

> A dagger of the mind, a false creation.
> (*Macb.* II. i. 38.)
> This is the very coinage of your brain:
> This bodiless creation ecstasy
> Is very cunning in. (*Ham.* III. iv. 138.)

Shelley refers in his *Defence of Poetry* to the 'bold and true words of Tasso: *non merita nome di creatore, se non Iddio ed il Poeta*,' and he repeats the phrase with some variation in a letter to Peacock of 16 August 1818. This, if Shelley quotes correctly, is an early use of *creatore* in connection with poetry; but none of Shelley's editors seem to have been able to find the source of the quotation. I have searched for it in vain in Tasso's works.

54. The Greek name of poet signifies, he says, 'Makers or Creators, such as raise admirable Frames and Fabricks out of nothing,' *Of Poetry* (1690) (Spingarn, vol. iii. p. 74). In his *Essay of Gardening* (1685) Temple describes building and gardening as 'a sort of Creation'.

55. On the *Pleasures of Imagination* (*Spectator*, No. 419, 1 July 1712).

56. *Spectator*, No. 421, 3 July 1712.

57. Edition of 1732, vol. iii. pp. 4, 5.

58. The notion that poetic creation was principally concerned with the creation of supernatural beings remained a commonplace of eighteenth-century criticism. Addison refers to it (with especial reference to Caliban) in the *Spectator* (No. 279); it is repeated by Joseph Warton (again with reference to Caliban) in an Essay in the *Adventurer* (No. 93). The German-Swiss critic Bodmer echoed it in Germany with reference to the angels 'created by Milton', and it found its way into the aesthetic criticism of Immanuel Kant. Hazlitt, in his *Characters of Shakespeare's Plays* (1817, p. 116), mentions Caliban and the supernatural element in *The Tempest* as the 'fantastic creation' of Shakespeare's mind.

59. 'This Divine, miraculous, creative power' (Cudworth's *Intellectual System*, 1678). Quoted *OED*.

60. *The Adventurer*, No. 93, 25 Sept. 1753.

61. Edition of 1871, vol. i. p. 93.
62. p. 48.
63. A very summary account of the history of *Genius* occupies fifty-two columns in Grimm's great German Dictionary (article *Genie*).
64. *Life of Cowley.*
65. G. Gregory Smith, vol. i. p. 195. Sidney goes on to quote the proverb, *Orator fit, Poeta nascitur.* This and the more common saying, *Poeta nascitur, non fit*, have not been traced further back than the fifteenth century. *Ibid.* p. 397.
66. Ker, vol. ii. p. 138.
67. *Ibid*, vol. i. p. 86.
68. *Answer to Davenant* (1650), Spingarn, vol. ii. p. 59.
69. *Ibid.* p. 25.
70. Ker, vol. i. p. 222. This absurd emendation (οὐ for ἤ) was borrowed, as Professor Ker points out, from the French critic, Rapin. *Ibid.* p. 318.
71. R. Wolseley, *Preface to Rochester's Valentinian* (1685), Spingarn, vol. iii. p. 12.
72. Sir William Alexander's *Anacrisis*, Spingarn, vol. i. p. 185.
73. Dennis in Nichol Smith, *Eighteenth-Century Essays on Shakespeare*, p. 24.
74. *On Poetry*, Spingarn, vol. iii. p. 48.
75. *Rambler*, No. 154, 7 Sept., 1751.
76. Reynolds's *Discourses*, ed. Fry, 1905, p. 175.
77. Among those which I have made use of in writing this paper may be mentioned:

    1751 Richard Hurd, *A Discourse concerning Poetical Imitation.* (In Hurd's edition of Horace's *Epistolae ad Pisones et Augustum*, vol. ii.)

    1754 Thomas Warton, *Observations on the Faerie Queene.*

    1755 William Sharpe, *A Dissertation upon Genius.*

    1756 Edmund Burke, *Philosophical Inquiry into the Origin of our Ideas of the Sublime and Beautiful.*

    1757 Joseph Warton, *An Essay on the Genius and Writings of Pope*, vol. i.

    1759 Edward Young, *Conjectures on Original Composition.*

    1762 Richard Hurd, *Letters on Chivalry and Romance.*

    1766 E. Capell, *Reflections on Originality in Authors.*

    1767 [W. Duff], *An Essay on Original Genius.*

    1769 Mrs Montagu, *An Essay on the Writings and Genius of Shakespeare.*

1769 Robert Wood, *An Essay on the Original Genius of Homer*.

1774 Alexander Gerard, *An Essay on Genius*.

78. In his *Discourse on Lyric Poetry* (1728), Young had already emphasized this notion that the methods, not the works, of the ancients, should be imitated.

79. Preface to the *Poems* of D. Triller, 1751. Quoted in Grimm's *Wörterbuch*, and more fully in Lessing's *Schriften* (1838), vol. iii. p. 214. Campe proposed *Schöpfergeist* ('creative spirit') as a translation for *genius* (Grimm, *Wörterbuch*).

80. Readers of Goethe's *Wahrheit und Dichtung* will remember how he embodied these watchwords in a witty address to a Leipzig baker:

> Who bakes
> With creative genius, original cakes.
> (*Du bäckst . . .*
> *Mit schöpfrischem Genie, originelle Kuchen*) (Book VII.)

German critics are agreed in tracing these watchwords and the ideas they embody to English sources, and above all to Young's *Conjectures* (see *Edward Young in Germany*, by J. L. Kind, New York, 1906).

From *Genie* the Germans coined the adjectives *genial* and *genialisch*, meaning 'characterized by genius' in its modern sense. Our word *genial* comes through the Latin *genialis*, from *genius*, meaning 'social enjoyment'. The French word *génial* is borrowed from German, with its German meaning.

81. *A History of English Romanticism in the Eighteenth Century*, by Henry A. Beers, London (1899), p. 422.

82. One of the pioneers of the medieval revival in England was Thomas Warton, Professor of Poetry at Oxford, a Poet Laureate in 1785. Professor Beers rightly calls attention to the interest, in the history of the English Romantic Movement, of his poem on Sir Joshua Reynolds's window in New College Chapel (published in 1784). Warton confesses that, 'a faithless truant to the classic page', he had loved to explore old mansions and castles, and Gothic churches,

> Where SUPERSTITION, with capricious hand
> In many a maze the wreathed window plann'd,
> With hues romantic ting'd the gorgeous pane,
> To fill with holy light the wondrous fane;

but then he goes on to tell how the 'chaste design' 'and just proportions of Reynolds's window disenchanted his cheated mind,

> Broke the Gothic chain
> And brought my bosom back to truth again.

He then urges, in manner of a palinode, that the brawny prophets, the bearded patriarchs, the virgins and angels, the martyrdoms and miracles of the Gothic glass, should

> No more the sacred window's round disgrace,
> But yield to Grecian groupes the shining space.

To visit New College Chapel with these verses, and attempt to re-capture the mood of this recantation, would be a useful exercise in the historical study of bygone ways of feeling. The same conflict is expressed by Horace Walpole's account of his feelings at Stowe. 'The Grecian Temple is glorious: this I openly worship: in the heretical corner of my heart I adore the Gothic building' (*Letters*, ed. Toynbee, vol. iii. p. 181). It is amusing to learn that Reynolds was not at all convinced of the genuineness of Warton's recantation. 'I owe you great obligations,' he wrote him, 'for the sacrifice which you have made, or pretend to have made, to modern art: I say pretend; for though it is allowed that you have, like a true poet, feigned marvellously well, and have opposed the two different styles with the skill of a Connoisseur, yet I may be allowed to entertain some doubts of the sincerity of your conversion. I have no great confidence in the recantation of such an old offender.' Thomas Warton, *Poetical Works* (1802), vol. i. pp. lxxx-i.

83. This distinction was noticed by Condillac in his *Essai sur l'origine des connaissances humaines* (1746), I. ii. par. 104, when, writing of invention, he says, 'Il y en a de deux espèces: le talent et le génie. Celui-là combine les idées d'un art ou d'une science connue, d'une manière propre à produire les effets qu'on en doit naturellement attendre ... Celui-ci ajoute au talent l'idée d'esprit, en quelque sorte, créateur. Il invente de nouveaux arts, ou, dans le même art, de nouveaux genres égaux ... Un homme à talent a un caractère qui peut appartenir à d'autres; ... Un homme de génie a un caractère original, il est inimit-able.'

The conception of Genius was the product of the whole movement of European thought; and to this France, as well as England and Germany, made its contribution. But the French conception was not as near to our modern conception as the above quotation would seem to indicate. The connection between imagination and genius was first suggested in England; in France genius was more connected with *esprit*. Condillac denied any real creative power to genius; its activity consisted for him in the power of combining in new relations the materials furnished by experience. This, he said, was invention. Genius possessed invention in a higher degree than talent; it was an *esprit simple* which was able to find what no one had ever been able to discover before (see L. Dewaule, *Condillac et la psychologie anglaise contemporaine* (1892), pp. 89– 90). The notions current in France on these subjects are embodied and discussed by Voltaire in his *Dictionnaire philosophique*, articles *Esprit*, *Génie, Imagination*, etc.

84. With regard to present usage, the *Oxford Dictionary* says, 'The difference between *genius* and *talent* has been formulated very variously by different writers, but there is general agreement in regarding the former as the higher of the two, as "creative" and "original", and as achieving its results by instinctive perception and spontaneous activity, rather than by processes which admit of being distinctly analyzed.'

85. The abstract terms *Romanticism* and *Classicism* are not found in English with the meanings they had acquired abroad till a later date (*Romanticism* 1844, *Classicism* 1837). The problems involved took the form, in the concrete English way, of a discussion as to whether Pope could be called a poet, and an attempt to establish an antithesis between magical and evocative poetry, as opposed to a rhetorical and didactic verse.

86. Review of Southey's *Thalaba*, Oct. 1802.

87. The first instance of the appellation *Lake School* which the *Oxford Dictionary* cites is from an article of Jeffrey's in the *Edinburgh Review* of Aug. 1817.

88. It would be interesting to discover when the English Romantic poets of the early nineteenth century were first all grouped together under this Anglo-Franco-German term. Writing in 1886, Alois Brandl remarked in his *Life of Coleridge* that the phrase 'Lake School' was a name, but not a designation, and suggested that this group of poets, with the addition of Scott (but not the more 'classical' Keats, Byron, and Shelley), should be called the English 'Romantic School' (English translation, p. 222). I do not know when first the Lake Poets were grouped together with Byron, Keats, Shelley, and Scott as 'Romantic Poets', but it must be fairly recent.

89. Brandl, in his *Life of Coleridge*, says that Coleridge derived the distinction he made between Genius and Talent ('Talent was manufacture, Genius a gift, that no labour or study could supply,' etc.) from his reading of Jean Paul Richter; and that also the famous distinction between Fancy and the 'higher and creative' faculty of Imagination was derived from the same source (Brandl, English translation, p. 316). However, this latter distinction had already been suggested by Dryden, who wrote, 'the first happiness of the poet's imagination is properly invention, or finding of the thought; the second is fancy, or the variation, deriving, or moulding of that thought' (Ker, vol. i. p. 15). The distinction, however, was not noticed by Dryden's contemporaries, nor did Dryden himself afterwards observe it. Addison explicitly stated in 1712 that he used *Fancy* and *Imagination* promiscuously (*Spectator*, No. 411). The distinction between the two was, however, elaborated by W. Duff in his *Essay on Original Genius* (1767) – a book that Coleridge must, I think, have read. 'Wit & Humour,' Duff writes, 'are produced by the efforts of a *rambling* and *sportive* Fancy, the latter [Genius] proceeds from the copious effusions of a plastic Imagination' (p. 52). 'A vigorous, extensive, and plastic Imagination is the principal qualification of the one [Genius], and a quick and lively Fancy the distinguishing characteristic of the other' (p. 58).

The distinction, also emphasized by Coleridge, between 'mechanical' and 'organic' – the products of Fancy and Talent being 'mechanical', those of Imagination and Genius being 'organic' – is also traced by Brandl to Coleridge's reading of Schlegel and Jean Paul Richter. It was Leibnitz who first suggested this distinction; its aesthetic application was worked out in Germany, although, as usual, we find it casually suggested in England in the eighteenth century, as when Young writes, 'an *original* may be said to be of a vegetable nature', etc. (see *ante*, p. 27). Young uses the word *mechanic*, but not the word *organic*. The first appearance which I have found of *organic* with this meaning is in Coleridge's *Lectures on Shakespeare* (delivered in 1810–11, and published in 1849), where he attributes the error of Voltaire's abuse of Shakespeare to 'the confounding of mechanical regularity with organic form' (ed. 1865, p. 54).

90. Of other additions to our vocabulary of criticism, perhaps the most important is the use of the old word *imaginative* with the meaning, as defined by the *OED* of 'characterized by, or resulting from, the productive Imgination; bearing evidence of high poetic or creative fancy.' The first quotation for this use given by the *OED* is from the

introduction to Scott's *Guy Mannering* in the edition of 1829. *Realism* as a term of art-criticism was used by Ruskin in 1856, *realistic* by Emerson in the same year, and *realist* by Swinburne in 1870.

91. German critics have ascribed to Schiller the first real appreciation of the aesthetic significance of music.

92. Shaftesbury refers to the harmony of music in his *Characteristicks* (Part III., 3), and Capell to the non-imitative arts, architecture and music, in his *Reflections on Originality* (1766).

93. The emergence of the words *taste* and *aesthetic* are other indications of this subjective trend in criticism. The use of *taste* to describe a 'special function of the mind' is generally attributed to the Spanish Jesuit Gracian (1601–58), and Addison ascribes the phrase 'the fine taste' to him (see Spingarn, vol. i. p. xcii.). The first instance of its use in English is in the line, quoted by the *OED* from *Paradise Regained*, 'Sion's songs, to all true tastes excelling' (iv. 347). *Aesthetic* is an invention of a German critic of the eighteenth century, Baumgarten. It is first found in English in 1798 (*OED*).

94. Fam'd be thy tutor, and thy parts of nature
    Thrice-fam'd, beyond all erudition

    (*Troilus and Cressida* II. iii. 256–7).

    So also Sir Henry Wotton writes of Essex, 'The Earl was of good Erudition, having been placed at Study in *Cambridge* very young' (quoted *OED*).

95. Quoted *OED*. So also the *OED* quotes from another writer, 'the Merit both of Intaglio's and Cameo's depends on their Erudition, on the Goodness of the Workmanship, and on the Beauty of their Polish.'

96. See *The Times*, 11 May 1914, p. 9.

97. *A Defence of Poetry.*

98. 'There is in genius itself an unconscious activity; nay, that is the genius in the man of genius.' Coleridge, *Essay on Poesy in Art* (*Biographia Literaria*, ed. Shawcross, vol. ii. p. 258). 'Talent differs from genius, as voluntary differs from involuntary power.' Hazlitt, *The Indian Jugglers, Table Talk*, vol. i. p. 195. 'The definition of genius is that it acts unconsciously; and those who have produced immortal works, have done so without knowing how or why. The greatest power operates unseen.' *Plain Speaker*, i. p. 284.

99. How much 'originality' we should find in the poem of Catullus, *ille mi par esse deo videtur*, did we not know that this poem was a direct translation from Sappho!

100. *Life of Waller.*
101. *Life of Pope.*
102. 'A long poem is a test of invention, which I take to be the Polar Star of Poetry, as Fancy is the Sails and Imagination the rudder.' *Letter* to Bailey, 8 Oct. 1817.
103. *Histoire du Romantisme*, p. 65.
104. *Biog. Lit.*, chap. xiii.
105. *Times Literary Supplement*, 20 Sept. 1917.
106. *Oxford Lectures on Poetry*, pp. 5, 6.
107. Herford, *The Age of Wordsworth*, p. 236.
108. *The Sense of Beauty*, p. 180.
109. *Poetry and Religion*, pp. 269–70.
110. *The Poetical Works of Robert Bridges* (1912), p. 191.

2: 'On Not Reading Shakespeare' & 'The Great Reward: Poetry'

from

On Reading Shakespeare (1933)

ON NOT READING SHAKESPEARE

——— ✳ ———

I

I AM not a Shakespeare scholar, nor am I a constant reader of his plays. I cannot say with Coleridge that no day of my life had passed without opening one or another of those volumes. I have, of course, read and re-read Shakespeare – there have been times in my life when this has been one of my main occupations. But intervals have often elapsed between these perusals; sometimes long intervals, when I haven't, it is true, forgotten Shakespeare – one cannot do that – but when a kind of resentment, a touch of exasperation, has kept my thoughts from the subject.

The truth is that the world's great writers are apt to become the world's great bores. We must put on our finest moods for their society, and these court-costumes of the soul are not comfortable for long. And then the Masters ask – or their admirers ask on their behalf – for more attention than we have time to give them. Homer, Virgil, Dante, Shakespeare – a whole life of study can be well devoted to each of these; and fate has vouchsafed us only one brief span of distracted existence. There is always the risk, too, that what begins as a taste may become an obsession. The works of great writers doze with their backs to us on our shelves for years, but they are dangerous company. Potent spirits lie imprisoned in those leather bottles. The names inscribed upon them are names which have defeated time, and may exert a formidable spell on us. Opening a volume of this kind in an idle ' moment, we may be seized upon, be-jinned and captured. We want only to look up a quotation perhaps in some old author, but we must go on, page after page, and then go on to read all the books we can find about him. The reader becomes a student, the student a bigot, and what is justly called a blind admirer, for his eyes are blinded by gazing on the object of his worship. Blemishes and merits are all blurred together, and faults seem to him perfections. Such a specialist is the last person in the world to give a measured and rational judgement on his special subject.

But there is a peril worse than this which we may encounter. The greatest writers of the world are enigmatic figures; they glimmer and loom in mists of controversy, and as

That Theban Monster that propos'd
Her riddle, and him, who solv'd it not, devour'd,

they propose problems to the world for which the world can find no answer. The question of Homer is enough to nonplus any student; but of the questionable shapes which may leap from our shelves and drag us off to their dens of dark obscurity, Dante and Shakespeare are more to be dreaded. But while Dante merely petrifies the brains of most Dante students, and turns them into pedants,[1] the attempt to solve the famous Shakespeare problem may deprive us altogether of our wits. And even if we escape this ultimate disaster, we shall find his figure, if we gaze too long upon it, grow to such proportions that other writers must be dwarfed and pushed aside.

The way, too, that Shakespeare has been made into a kind of national institution tends to make us hostile and suspicious; we feel inclined, as a recent critic has said, to tap the pedestal of this imposing statue; and gazing up at its vacuous face, we ask ourselves whether we are not, after all, being hoaxed. And when we do open a Shakespeare play, what rant we often find ourselves reading, what doggerel and dull jokes, what tedious writing! How the crude horseplay bores in the comedies, the hackneyed situation repeated over and over, the mirthless puns, and the intolerable chop-logic passing itself off as wit! What swollen rhetoric abounds in the historical plays, and how we are deafened by all the drum-and-trumpet business! The tragedies are full of melodrama, and holocausts of slaughter, and end, as Tolstoy said, with the dragging out by their legs of half-a-dozen corpses. How can we help feeling at times that 'repulsion, weariness and bewilderment', which Tolstoy tells us he always felt when he read Shakespeare? The famous 'What? What?' of George III will sometimes echo in our ears. Was there ever in fact, as the Patriot King unpatriotically asked, 'such stuff as a great part of Shakespeare? Only,' he added 'one must not say so.' But this crowned Shakespearean critic (who afterwards went mad) did say it. 'What! is there not sad stuff? What? What?' he barked at Fanny Burney.

Is there not indeed sad stuff? Must its writer be seriously regarded as the noblest of all poets, the glory of human nature, the greatest mind that has ever appeared among men, and the 'perfect boast of time'? This barbaric medley of bombast and ribaldry, of blood and melo-drama – is this really the top of human achievement, the noblest memorial, as we are told, that our race can leave behind it of our existence on this planet? Can it be, as a great thinker has conjectured, that in their celestial colloquies the high authorities of the universe call the earth 'Shakespeare', from the glory shed upon it by his genius which flashes afar through the interstellar spaces?

Can these things be? Or are we imposed upon, hocussed and bamboozled, the dupes of a gigantic Brocken-spectre of make-believe and mist, and victims, as Tolstoy so impressively maintained,[2] of a great collective hallucination, one of those crazes and epidemic manias, like the belief in witches or in the approaching end of the world, by which whole nations and whole ages have often been obsessed? Even the high priests of this established Shakespeare wor-ship seem to betray, now and then, an uneasy consciousness of something equivocal about the object of their devotion; of things to be hushed up, and the need of whitewash.

II

The statue, indeed, looks all right – there he stands, 'our Shakespeare', the great poet of Great Britain, and the volume he holds belongs, with the English Bible and the English Prayer Book, to the most sacred possessions of our race. In it we find the record of his genius, so myriad-minded and yet so English, with his joy in the English country-side and his appreciation of the bluff, honest qualities which make the inhabitants of this island what they are. He has, indeed, suffered much, has been through a time when the sorrows of the world have pressed heavily on his soul; but even in this dark period he never lost the fundamental sanity of his view of life; and his last years were spent in an atmosphere of reconciliation and quiet happiness, in the golden glow of an opulent and serene sunset of the spirit.

But the whitewash, alas, will keep flaking off and leave unsightly patches – the money-lending, for instance, and the petty lawsuits which occupied that evening of his years, and the second-best bed he bequeathed to his wife, as an afterthought, just when his sun was about to set. We can explain away this bed of his last bequest; we can also explain away his hurried marriage to its occupant in his youth; but what are we to do about those sonnets he was fond of writing, his brutal sonnets to the Dark Lady, and his sentimental sonnets to the Lovely Boy? The story Shakespeare recounts of his moral – or rather his immoral – predicament between these 'two loves' of his –

Two loves I have of comfort and despair –

must certainly, in the interests of the British Empire, be smothered up; the business of proving and re-proving, and proving over again – and then proving still once more, just to be absolutely certain – that our Shakespeare cannot possibly mean what he so frankly tells us, has become almost a national industry.

And then, too, there is Shakespeare's ribaldry – the bawdy jokes he is so fond of making. Luckily, it is only the specialist who knows how much ribaldry there is in Shakespeare's plays, how many passages which seem innocent enough are full of double-meanings. 'He can't mean that!' the shocked reader exclaims; but oh, my dear reader, he does mean it, and his meaning, if you are a nice-minded person, will make you blush all over. The late Poet Laureate tried to palliate the offence on the ground that Shakespeare was compelled against his will to season in this gross way the plays he wrote for his gross audience; but Robert Bridges did not explain the recondite improprieties which must have been far above the vulgar apprehension, and the indelicacies with which he spiced the sugared sonnets written for his private friends. A gross age, no doubt, but Sidney and Spenser wrote no sonnets of this kind. Even worse than this ithyphallic fun in which Shakespeare so plainly delighted, is the evidence of a more distressing kind of sex-preoccupation, by which, during a certain period of his life, he seems to have been obsessed. Lear's obscene railings against the mere fact of sex, which are quite inappropriate to his circumstances and situation, and in which he seems to scream and spit from horror, and Timon's even more terrible outbursts of sex-nausea, sound like the incoherent ravings of an unbalanced mind, driven to madness by a loathing for men and women in their natural intercourse together.

Difficult also to explain away is the moral callousness which Shakespeare often shows, not only in the physical atrocities he sometimes exhibits on the stage – the 'Out, vile jelly!' for instance, of Gloster's blinding – but in the moral outrages he perpetrates upon our feelings – the way he pardons, or rather ignores, unpardonable things; mates his heroines to dastards, and brings more than one of his plays by an ugly bed-trick to an ugly conclusion.[3]

It is impossible to get rid of the suspicion that of all great artists Shakespeare was the most completely devoid of all artistic conscience; that he was perfectly willing to make any sacrifice for the sake of stage-effect, money, and popular applause. One cannot but think of him and the other Elizabethan dramatists as being not unlike pastry-cooks who concoct their pies with little thought of anything but their sale to the customer of the day, and who are not in the least scrupulous about the ingredients they put into them.

III

The fact is well known that writing for the stage was not regarded as literature in Shakespeare's time. The drama existed to supply that popular demand for mental recreation which sates itself today with newspaper, magazines, murder stories and the cinema; and new plays, hot and hot, were constantly needed. A play, however successful, never had a 'run', and was repeated at the most seven or eight times a year. They were regarded for the most part as being of but ephemeral interest; and though, like sermons, one might be occasionally printed, the greater part of them have probably perished; the less than seven hundred Elizabethan plays which survive probably representing but a small proportion of those which were written, and even of those which were produced. Their writers, who had to furnish them as fast as they were needed, much as a modern journalist has to furnish a certain amount of copy at a certain date, worked in haste, and had small time for revision; and once paid for their work, did not as a rule trouble themselves about the fate of their compositions. Not literary reputation, but the crowded theatre was their reward.

What an amazing phenomenon by the way is the Elizabethan drama! This sudden outburst of passionate, imaginative rhetoric and unbounded poetic imagination, which flared up for so brief a period, and in twenty years passed, as it has been said, 'from the fiery dawn of Marlowe to the silvered dusk of Massinger' – what literary phenomenon in our own, or in any literary history is comparable in its strangeness and splendour to this? Sir Walter Raleigh gives a most vivid picture of it in his *Shakespeare*; how the beginnings of popular drama already existed in the London of the eighties, with its clowns and jugglers and players and authors of dramatic interludes, who had grown prosperous by their popular success; and how this flaunting underworld was invaded by a band of reckless young men from the universities, not scholars in any strict sense, but 'who had been caught by the Latin poets, and were eager students of the new literature of the Renaissance in Italy, France, and Spain.' They came to live by their wits in London, first of all as hack-writers for the booksellers; but they soon became acquainted with the flaunting vagabonds of the stage, the 'harlotry players', as Mrs Quickly called them, who were both actors and dramatic writers, and who, finding their old interludes and Morality Plays falling out of fashion, felt there was room for the new inventions of these scholars; took them to live among them, and made them acquainted with the 'lewdest persons of the land'.

Of these university men Marlowe was the king; 'already, before his arrival, Lyly had shown the way to make classical mythology engaging, and Peele had used blank verse so that it rang in the ear and dwelt in the memory.' But 'the work of these men was designed for select courtly circles, and left the wider public untouched. Marlowe appealed to the people. He brought blank verse on to the public stage and sent it echoing through the town.' Marlowe not only made classical fable popular, but he imagined great and serious actions and splendid passions and heroic characters. The success of his *Tamburlaine* in 1587 is perhaps, Sir Walter Raleigh says, the greatest event in our literary history. His friends and fellows, Peele and Greene and

Nashe, recognized his triumph, and followed his lead to claim a share in his success. Out they poured it all, stately masques, and Italianate, Arcadian Pastorals, comedy, coarseness, ribaldry and splendid declamation, and above all that world of terror and horror, which in the ancient and Renaissance theatre was by prescription allotted to tragedy. 'The mandates and kings', as the phrase of Scaliger has it, 'slaughters, despairs, executions, exiles, loss of parents, parricides, incests, conflagrations, battles, loss of sight, tears, shrieks, lamentations, burials, epitaphs and funeral songs.'[4]

What a seething cauldron of blood, ghosts, horror, grossness and splendid poetry it all is!

If we want to catch the thrill of witnessing such a drama in the 'wooden O', as Shakespeare calls it, the 'round', the 'ring', 'Cock-pit', of a little old theatre, long ago, one winter day in London, we shall find it most vividly described in Marston's famous Prologue to *Antonio's Revenge*, when, after describing the dank of 'clumsy' winter, with its sleet and snarling gusts, he adds,

> O now, methinks, a sullen tragic scene
> Would suit the time with pleasing congruence . . .
>   Therefore, we proclaim,
> If any spirit breathes within this round,
> Uncapable of weighty passion, . . .
> Who winks, and shuts his apprehension up
> From common sense of what men were and are,
> Who would not know what men must be — let such
> Hurry amain from our black-visaged shows:
> We shall affright their eyes. But if a breast
> Nail'd to the earth with grief; if any heart
> Pierc'd through with anguish pant within this ring;
> If there be any blood whose heat is choked
> And stifled with true sense of misery;
> If ought of these strains fill this consort up —
> Th' arrive most welcome.

But what now remains of all this sudden brief blaze of poetry, rhetoric and passion? Lamb and our romantic critics revelled in it, but the world has found it for the most part too wild, chaotic, noisy and incoherent, too lacking in restraint and intellectual substance, to win for itself, in spite of Marlowe, Webster, Ford, Dekker, Heywood and the others, an assured place with the Greek, the French, and even with the Spanish drama, in the literature of the world. It blazed up and it died down; the intellectuals of the time paid no serious attention to it, and today only a few readers and scholars rake over, now and then, its still-fiery ashes. For us its real interest is the splendid accident of Shakespeare's appearance, which glorified the Elizabethan drama, and yet in a way robbed it of its glory; the way he shone out and eclipsed those fellow playwrights of his; 'how far,' in Lamb's phrase, 'in his divine mind and manners he surpassed them and all mankind.' But one thing may be said, that to understand Shakespeare's greatness, and to what heights he soars above his contemporaries, it pays, or almost pays, a person of infinite astronomical leisure like myself to read, as I have read, the Elizabethan drama as a preliminary to reading Shakespeare; to explore first the foothills from among which that great summit rises.

IV

Ben Jonson was the only dramatic writer of that time who, with the exception perhaps of Lyly, was blessed, or (as it has been suggested) cursed with an artistic conscience, and who had any feeling for the dignity of his profession, or solicitude about the future of his plays. His fellows ridiculed him for the time and toil he gave to his compositions; and when he published them in 1616, he confounded both his friends and enemies by the audacity of calling them his *Works* on the title page. Works! So grave, so stately, so dignified a title, reserved for great classical writers, great scholars, and grave theologians, printed on the title-page of a collection of mere stage-plays! The indignation and laughter lasted for many years, and the editors of Shakespeare did not dare to use the word on the title-page of the Folio, and only insinuated it on a later page, where it was not likely to attract any general attention.

These editors praise Shakespeare for his haste in composition; he had never blotted a line they declared proudly ('Would he had blotted a thousand!' Ben Jonson retorts). In fact, although Shakespeare took his long poems seriously, and saw to their careful printing, he does not seem to have regarded his plays as serious performances, and to have taken any pride in acknowledging them – indeed, the first editions of his separate plays were published anonymously, and to the printing of none of the quartos which came out in his lifetime did he give the least attention.[4]

V

It is no considerations of the kind which I have been writing, however, which make me hesitate before reading Shakespeare. His hasty composition and hasty marriage do not disconcert me, nor the money-lending nor the bedstead; I don't mind the ribaldry, I rather like it,[5] and in the Sonnets I find described a sex-quandary which psycho-analysis has taught us to regard as not at all unusual. Although, as a matter of personal taste, I love best those artists who, like Virgil or Milton, love and respect their art, and seek to attain perfection in it, I am not too narrow-minded to enjoy the careless prodigality of the great purveyors who employ their divine gifts in catering for the public. Great art is great art, in whatever workshop it is fashioned and for however mercenary a purpose. Molière and Scott and Dickens wrote for the market, and many of the immortal painters of the Renaissance actually kept shops, in which they turned out their masterpieces in the ordinary way of business.

What, however, does make me uneasy is a certain misgiving – not about Shakespeare, but about myself. Granted that his work deserves all the praise which has been lavished on it, are we in the fitting mood just now to appreciate that splendour? We are all the children of our age: we cannot help it; and in the East wind which prevails today have we the high spirits to enjoy Shakespeare's boisterous fun? Shall we not find our ears out of tune for his sweet music; and may not his pretty boy-and-girl romances seem rather insipid to our taste? And, above all, will his pathos still move us; and if it does move us, may it not be in a way that we resent?

Pathos, the power of touching our tender feelings, has always been one of the great gifts of the greatest writers; there is noble pathos in Homer, in Virgil, and in Dante, and again and again in the voices of the most famous novelists the sound of a sob is heard.[7] None of our modern writers dare, however, to touch that string: we are lacking in the sensibility which responds with gratitude to such appeals. Now Shakespeare is certainly the most moving of all writers, the greatest master of pathos the world has ever known. No one can unlock the source of tears and wring the heart as he wrings it; and I must confess that I find the harrowing scenes in Shakespeare, like the scene between Arthur and Hubert in *King John*, or the slaughter of Macduff's children, or the deaths of Lear and Desdemona, intolerable – I cannot bear them; and even scenes which are not quite so harrowing: Desdemona's Willow Songs, for instance, or Ophelia's madness, I find 'shy-making', to use a new-invented phrase.

Perhaps the Elizabethans were made of sterner stuff than we are, and did not mind being hit below the belt; or perhaps they wore their belts lower than we wear them. Or it may be that our inability to enjoy such appeals to the emotions is due to some temporary exasperation of the spirit from which the spirit will recover? Or, I sometimes wonder, may it not be the inevitable effect of modern science on our modern world-outlook? If remorse and agony and vehement passion are regarded no longer as moral, but as pathological phenomena, how can those who so regard them be moved by the pity and terror on which, as Aristotle said, tragedy is based? With the loss of our belief in the responsibility of the free agent, have we lost also the tragic sense of life? We may feel that life is meaningless and hateful, we may be exasperated to desperation by it; but when from our desolate vision of the cosmos we turn to the glowing and highly-coloured world of Shakespeare's, the poet of Free Will, full as it is of moral tragedies and triumphs, of vehement will and ardour and agony, may it not seem a tempest in an inconsiderable cup which it is superfluous for us to augment with our tears?

VI

All these fine reasons which I allege to myself for not reading
Shakespeare are, however, I know quite well, little more than ration-
alizations, as they are called, of indolence; high-sounding excuses in
which my dread of the difficulty of the task seeks to hide its head. For
plays, unlike novels, demand close attention, they demand a certain
effort of the mind and the imagination; and Shakespeare's plays,
above all, require study: his vocabulary is full of obsolete words and
idioms; and his writing, especially in the later plays, is sometimes so
involved and obscure, so rapid and abrupt, that we cannot understand
it. To read and only half-comprehend what one is reading hardly
seems a satisfactory method of perusal; while to pause and consult a
glossary and pore over one note after another fatigues and distracts the
attention. And even these notes of the annotators will often add to our
embarrassment. Every line and every word in the text of Shakespeare
has been exposed to the fiercest light of criticism; and his commen-
tators have discovered, for the confusion of the perplexed reader,
almost innumerable difficulties which he would never have noticed for
himself.

> Thy tooth is not so keen,
> Because thou art not seen –

when Amiens addresses the winter wind in these words, or when Feste
sings:

> Then come kiss me, sweet and twenty,

or the Duke, in *Twelfth Night*, says of music:

> Give me excess of it, that, surfeiting,
> The appetite may sicken, and so die,

the common reader is perplexed to learn that these simple lines present
problems difficult to solve, and that when Kent threatens to make a
'sop o' the moonshine' of Goneril's steward, when Hamlet calls the

King 'a pajock', or Theseus speaks of his 'sanded' hounds, or Lorenzo of the 'patines of bright gold' which inlay the floor of heaven, no one knows for certain what they mean.

And we are told, also, that when we think we are reading Shakespeare we may not be reading him at all. His authorship of several of the plays assigned to him is doubtful; and even of those which are esteemed the most authentic we possess no authentic text, and cannot be sure of the accuracy of a single line. They have come down to us in a state of manifest and admitted corruption: all we possess is a set of prompt-books used by a particular troupe of actors for a particular audience. And, worse than all this, the view has come to be widely held that Shakespeare seldom wrote original plays: that it was his business rather to recast and furbish up old plays already in the repertory of his theatre; and that in the text of these, as we possess them, there remains not only much of the writing of their first authors, but layer after layer of subsequent additions. How far this process of disintegration of Shakespeare's text is a valid one, and to what results it may lead us, no one at present can possibly say. The battle between the disintegrators and the defenders of the accepted text, 'foliolators, growing desperate in their doomed undertaking' – so they are de-scribed by their opponents – is raging just now more fiercely than ever.

Even more formidable are the barriers which another set of critics have erected between Shakespeare and his readers. Shakespeare's plays, they tell us, were not written to be read, but acted, and to read them is to miss their true significance and meaning. They are perform-ances, designed for the eyes and ears of their spectators, moving pageants of action, sound, and colour; the texts we possess are like operatic scores; to read one of these is at the best but reading the score of an opera and trying to hum its tunes. And even if we do succeed in re-creating in imagination the play as a stage performance, our difficulties are by no means over. The stage of Shakespeare's time was so totally different from the stage as we know it, that we distort and disfigure his plays if we place them upon our stage, whether in imagination or actual performance. To understand Shakespeare, therefore, we must fit ourselves out with Elizabethan eyes and ears; must stand beneath the open sky in an enclosure hardly larger than a tennis-court, 'to see a boy-Lady Macbeth act before a curtain declaring itself to be a royal palace'. We must in fact reconstruct for ourselves the Elizabethan stage, and master the art of stagecraft as it was practised in Shakespeare's time. But as this is at present impossible, and, indeed, may always be so, since our knowledge of the Elizabethan stage is, and is likely to remain, very incomplete, any attempt to re-create the tunes of Shakespeare's scores is like an attempt to recover the music of ancient instruments without knowing what sounds they actually did emit.

But this is by no means the worst of our predicament. As the approach to the great temples of Egypt is guarded by avenues of lions with human faces, who are supposed to tear their enemies to pieces, so the approach to the temple of Shakespeare-worship is beset by sphinxes who are quite as ready to dismember and devour those who give wrong answers to their questions. Of all the sphinxes of the East, the biggest of course is that great monster, 190 feet long, of Gizah, which gazes across the Valley of the Nile, and guards the entrance to it; almost as formidable to me is a modern monster of the Middle West which has recently heaved up her bulk in America, and stands with her avenue of daughter-sphinxes, gazing across the Mississippi Valley. For, according to this newborn school of critics, we must, if we wish to understand Shakespeare and the problems he presents, not only fit our heads with Elizabethan eyes and ears, but must furnish them inside with Elizabethan brains as well. The modern idea of Shakespeare, according to these critics, is nothing but a windy, vast balloon, inflated by German and Scotch professors, by literary gents of leisure, minor poets and writes of closet-plays ('let rude ears,' as Milton somewhere says, 'be absent'), by propagandists, idealists and blatherskites, who have combined to distend and blow it up with the hot air of modern transcendentalism, sentimentality, psychology and introspection – all things of which, of course, the Elizabethans had not the slightest notion. Shakespeare was one of these Elizabethans; he was not 'a prophet, living in the spirit of the nineteenth century while working in the sixteenth'; not a thinker voyaging through strange seas of thought alone, but a jolly old actor and playwright, who filled his borrowed plots with fine acting parts and thrilling situations, all concocted to suit the taste and temper of the time. To understand them we must understand that taste and temper, and realize that the meaning of these plays – their only meaning – is their surface meaning, as Shakespeare's contemporaries understood it. Shakespeare in writing his plays had in fact, they say, no subtle intentions and no deep underlying ideas; his characters were little more than the stock figures of the renascence stage. Falstaff is, and was meant to be a coward, a liar and boaster, 'a false, fat, tavern rogue, dissolute, scurillous and worthless'; Shylock is the hated Jew, and butt of the time, meant to be mocked at, spat upon, and dismissed at last with vindictive laughter and contempt. That Othello falls a prey at once to Iago's calumnies is not in the least due to any tragic flaw in his character, but simply to the universally accepted stage-convention that the calumniator is always believed at once, however incredible his calumnies may be. This can be proved, they say, by instances out of the whole history of the drama, from the age of Greece down to the nineteenth century; and indeed, according to this school, the great sin of criticism is to judge works of art, not by other works of art, but by life, with which they have little or no connection. In fact all the profound or mystical meanings we read into Shakespeare's plays are absurd anachronisms, about as irrelevant and absurd as the mystical relations between Christ and his spouse, the Church, which theologians read into those outspoken old erotic lyrics collected in the *Song of Songs*.

The leader of this American and hardest-boiled of all the hard-boiled schools of Shakespeare criticism, is a learned and out-spoken American professor, Professor Elmer Edgar Stoll, Ph.D., of Minneapolis, on the Mississippi River.[7] Professor Stoll is one of the most erudite of living Shakespeare scholars, and possesses also an accurate and unrivalled knowledge of dramatic history – of the Greek, the Latin, the Spanish, the Italian, the French and English theatres, and his scholarship is accompanied, as all sound scholarship should be accompanied, by a vigorous gift of invective; it is he, for instance, who has added to the vocabulary of Shakespearean criticism the word 'blatherskite' – 'a talker of blatant nonsense', as the dictionary defines it. I have incorporated above into my genteel prose, one or two of his less striking phrases. Altogether an awkward customer, a fierce eagle in the fluttered dovecotes, a wolf in the quiet fold of literary professors, and one who is moved to derision and no pity by their cooings and transcendental bleatings. And yet, as the erudite historian of

Shakespeare criticism admits with the sigh of one who prefers the old romantic method – Professor Stoll, whom he describes as among the first of contemporary critics, is, with his business-like methods, 'pointing the highway to the best criticism of the future'.[8]

VII

Many are the problems, as we have seen, both of text and interpretation, that meet the would-be reader of Shakespeare's plays. Of these problems, these Theban monsters threatening to devour those who cannot solve their riddles, two there are which have always perplexed me most, for the great Sonnet Problem I refuse to face. 'There are so many footprints,' as Sir Walter Raleigh grimly remarks, 'around the cave of this mystery, none of them pointing in the outward direction.' The first of these is what is called the Dark Period Problem, and the relation in general between Shakespeare's life and his plays; and the second is the problem of stage-representation – whether we best appreciate these plays by reading them, or by watching their performance on the stage. I hope, before I finish this essay, to try to face these two monsters, but in the meantime, Professor Stoll has raised a still more (to me at least) perplexing problem. Is it true, he makes us ask ourselves, that to understand and appreciate Shakespeare we must pop him back into his own age, judge his plays by the plays of his contemporaries and see life through the eyes with which he and they saw it? Is it not the business of the critic to help the reader to become the contemporary of the writer whose works he is reading, rather than to alchemize and etherealize and sentimentalize those works into contemporary writings? Can they possess beauties of which their author had no notion, and above all ideas that were perfectly unknown both to himself and to the age he lived in? Should we not then search for the truth, rather than invent and seek to impart it, and study Shakespeare, not by the light of modern, personal, temperamental impressions, which may mean anything, everything – which may mean nothing at all – but, sacrificing on the altar of sacred truth, all this 'sentimental finery', as our Professor calls it, read Shakespeare's plays only and austerely by the light, so dim to us, by which, after long research, we have come to believe he wrote them?

How shall I face this and the other Theban monsters, how answer their dark riddles and not be eaten up?

I have found it. Oh, happy answer! Why read Shakespeare at all? No one else reads him; why should I alone be forced to undertake the task? There is nothing about it in the Ten Commandments; no Voice from Mount Sinai has put this obligation on me; and if such a voice should shout it in my ears, could I not justifiably reply that the thing is impossible in the present state of things?

That just simply it can't be done?

And as for writing about Shakespeare, heaven preserve me from so mad and desperate an undertaking! Am I to climb all the insuperable fences, push my way through the impenetrable thickets, defy these formidable Sphinxes, only to have 'Blatherskite' shouted at me from the Middle West?

Let me alone, let me enjoy in peace my comforts and declining years. And anyhow, what with the brevity of those years, and with bridge, and going out to lunch, and all the modern murder-stories to occupy my so-called mind at home, how in heaven's name can I ever find time to read Shakespeare?

VIII

In one of his letters Henry James describes how ignobly fond he had become as he grew older of not travelling; 'to keep up not doing it,' he writes, 'is in itself for me the most thrilling of adventures.' So not to read Shakespeare, not to travel into his kingdom, but to sneak up at night towards the barriers that guard its frontier, and lurk there, terrified by the thought of the dangers I might encounter if I did really enter it, has become for me also a thrilling if not very noble adventure.

It may sound absurd to speak of danger in connection with a region which, in spite of a few geographical uncertainties, is so written up in handbooks, so betrod by tourists, so well provided with beaten roads and signposts and official guides. But it is a region, nevertheless, full of dark pitfalls for the mind; tangled thickets there are of significant, as well as textual interpretation; mazes of thought in which many wander and find no issue, and many paths whitened by the bleaching bones of critics. On one side of the beaten track, with its charabancs full of tourists, its files of boys and girls from the secondary schools, personally conducted by their teachers, lies the abyss I have mentioned of the great Dark Period; on the other, the Serbonian sonnet-bog, in which armies whole have sunk; while the attempt to reconcile the poetry which Shakespeare wrote with the prose of the extremely prosaic life he led is apt to addle the brains of those who undertake it. Shaken and appalled by the thought of this Apollo as an actor and jovial stage-manager in a little old London theatre – a mere bare room with a blanket for a curtain – this demi-god serenely running a popular show and raking in the pennies – this thought stupefies them, and they are seized with a kind of vertigo. Of the inhabitants of the insane asylums of Great Britain it has been calculated that, after the religious maniacs, the two next largest classes consist of those who rave about the Royal Family, or those who, by thinking about Shakespeare, have unhinged their minds.

A great divine of the Elizabethan age describes in one of his sermons a region in the East, in Georgia, which was so immersed all day in gloom that no one could see his own hand within its borders; those who dwelt upon its frontiers could hear, he said, the noise of cocks crowing, horses neighing, and the cries of human beings, but no one outside dared to venture in for fear of losing his way in that land of eternal darkness. Thus the cries of the distracted inhabitants sometimes reach us from the dark realm of Shakespeare interpretation. We hear the bleating of idiot adorers and the eternal swish of their whitewash brushes; we hear the squeals of the idealists and blatherskites as Professor Stoll pigsticks them; the war-cries of the Foliolaters and Disintegrators as they rush upon each other; and even wilder battle cries than these (for it is impossible to exaggerate their strangeness) will reach our ears. For listen! the fanatic followers of no less than five ghostly, resurrected Elizabethan Earls are shouting at each other, the two bands of Pembrokians and Southamptonites, each vociferating that their Lord was the inspirer of the Sonnets, while three other bands proclaim the more glorious boast (at least more glorious to some thinkers) that Lord Derby, or Lord Rutland, or Lord Oxford, was the author of them, and of Shakespeare's plays as well. And then, faint and far, as the wind shifts, we hear the ululations of those vaster herds of Baconian believers, as they plunge squeaking down the Gadarene slope of their delusion.[9]

Yes, on the whole I feel that I am against Shakespeare – the vast subject is too vexatious, too intricate and baffling. Though I may not join with Tolstoy and Bernard Shaw, and shout 'Down with Shakespeare!' in the streets, I shall nevertheless keep well aloof from the grounds of that great lunatic asylum, that dark domain of ghosts and pedants, of blatherskites, monomaniacs, fanatics and fools.

1. But Dante can be more dangerous sometimes; thus William Rossetti tells us how not only his father's mind, but his father's house in Charlotte Street was haunted by Dante as by a banshee, whose shriekings, however, had grown so familiar to the Rossetti children that they ceased to listen to them.

2. Tolstoy's essay is published in *Tolstoy and Art* (Oxford Press). There can be no question of the complete sincerity of this very able anti-Shakespeare manifesto, in which Tolstoy describes the astonishment and consternation with which he, on reading Shakespeare's plays, had always found himself in complete disagreement with the received opinion of their merits. He had read them again and again, he tells us; read them in English, read them in Russian and German translations; had discussed them over and over with Shakespeare enthusiasts, and at last, after a still more careful reperusal, he had found himself at the age of seventy-five faced with the alternative that either he or the world was mad, and had arrived at the 'final, indubitable, firm conviction,' that the world, with regard to Shakespeare, was the victim of one of those insane delusions, to which it always had been and always will be subject. Those deifications of Shakespeare he regarded (though he died before the War) as a piece of German propaganda, having been started by the German romantic writers for the purpose of liberating their drama from the tyranny of French ideals, thus substituting Shakespeare as a model which would leave them free to follow their own disorderly instincts and devices.

3. A list of the atrocities, the offences against taste, morals, and any kind of decent feeling, which are to be found in the canon of the Folio, and which

are accepted as Shakespeare's work by his adorers, is enough to prove – if more proof were needed – what enormities the orthodox can swallow, apparently without a gulp, in their Sacred Writings. Otherwise the belief that Shakespeare wrote that disgusting record of more than beastly horror, *Titus Andronicus*, within a year or so of writing *A Midsummer Night's Dream*, would burst their brains; nor would they find it easy to digest Shakespeare's treatment of Joan of Arc in the scene (I *Henry VI*, V, iv) where the Maid of France, to escape burning, declares herself to be with child, first by one, and then by another of the French Princes. The wager of Posthumus about the chastity of Imogen, the slaughter of the unarmed Hector at the instigation of Achilles in *Troilus and Cressida*, and indeed the ugly degradation of all the Greek heroes in that magnificent but unpleasant play, would turn the stomachs of less devout readers. The marriage of Celia to that scoundrel Oliver, in *As You Like It*, and that of Hero to the despicable Claudio in *Much Ado*, are bad enough, but as an outrage on our moral feelings few things in literature can equal the scene in the *Two Gentlemen of Verona*, where Valentine makes an outrageous and calm offer of Silvia, whom he loves, to the scoundrel whose attempt to outrage her he has just prevented. Shakespeare was apt to end off his plays, it is true, by any unscrupulous contrivance, but this plea can hardly be urged to palliate the cold-blooded rejection of Falstaff; and the only excuse which can be found for the degradation of that master-spirit into the poor dupe and buffoon of the *Merry Wives*, is to label as 'sentimentalists' those who do not like it.

4. I don't pretend that I have read Scaliger, or that I ever shall. I have borrowed this quotation from Professor Stoll's *Hamlet*, p. 65 n.

5. For the above account of the drama in Shakespeare's time, I am indebted to Professor Lounsbury's brilliant and fascinating book, *The First Editors of Shakespeare* (David Nutt, 1906).

6. That is, when I can understand it, which is by no means always easy. Thus the orchard scene in *Romeo and Juliet*, when Juliet rebukes Romeo for swearing by 'the moon, the inconstant moon' – this most exquisite of scenes is prefaced by a speech of Mercutio's full of double-meanings which the most earnest and impure-minded thinkers find it difficult to understand. Even when I was able at last to sit under the medlar tree and join in the learned giggles about

> That kind of fruit
> As maids call medlars, when they laugh alone,

I was for a long time baffled by the two lines which follow – lines held to be so atrocious that they are the only ones omitted in several otherwise unexpurgated editions of Shakepeare's plays. The best course for those seriously interested in this branch of Shakespearean research, is to study the notes of some frank eighteenth-century edition, or collate our modern text with the Bowdlerized text of the wily old Bowdler, and notice the passages he omits or changes. The keenness of Bowdler's wicked old nose has deservedly won for his name a place in our English vocabulary.

7. How highly this gift of pathos was esteemed by the Victorian novelists is illustrated by an anecdote which Leslie Stephen recounts with no ironic intention. When George Eliot, he tells us, had shown in her first story that she could write good dialogue, it was still a question whether she had the command of pathos. The doubt was settled, however, by her description of the last illness of Mrs Barton. She and Lewes both wept over this scene, and Lewes kissed her, exclaiming: 'I think your pathos is better than your fun.'

8. Professor Stoll has published one volume on Shakespeare, *Shakespeare Studies* (The Macmillan Company, N.Y., 1927), and several papers of importance, *Anachronism in Shakespeare Criticism* (Modern Philology, 1918), *Othello*, in the *Studies of Language and Literature* of the University of Minnesota, 1915, and *Hamlet*, in the same (1919), and *The Tempest*, in the Publications of the Modern Language Association of America (September, 1932). His latest volume, *Poets and Playwrights* (University of Minnesota Press), contains several essays on Shakespeare of great interest.

9. *Shakespearian Criticism*, Augustus Ralli, Oxford Press, Vol. II, p. 258.

10. I do not wish, however, to speak with any disrespect of that view of the authorship of Shakespeare's plays which is so firmly held by officers in the Navy and the Army, by one of His Majesty's judges, and the manager of more than one large drapery establishment, and is corroborated by the authority of Mark Twain, Mrs Henry Pott, Prince Bismarck, John Bright, the late Mr Crump, K.C., and several thoughtful baronets.

THE GREAT REWARD. I. POETRY

— ✳ —

I

Now that I have returned from the journey into Shakespeare's world, this plunge into the sea of books which surrounds that world, I feel impelled, like other travellers and voyagers, to exhibit the spoils I have brought back with me. No one, it has been said, should write about Shakespeare without a special licence; but although I do not hope to procure any such licence from the pundits, I cannot resist the temptation to describe the impression which this adventure has left upon me. I shall at least clarify my own experience; and my unlicensed essay may be of use to other unprofessional readers like myself. Many people, as it has been said, read in Shakespeare, but few really read him; but I at least have performed this feat.

To anyone who reads the works of Shakespeare in their chrono-logical order, from 1592, when at the age of twenty-eight he began, as far as we know for certain, to write, till the date (1607) of *Antony and Cleopatra* (for after this date his five remaining years of authorship show a certain decline, amidst all their splendour) – to any such reader the first impression must be that he has watched a growth of genius more astounding than any other which the world ever witnessed. In this supreme period of fifteen years – and Sainte-Beuve has defined the span of fifteen years as the period in the life of a great genius during which he produces his greatest work – in this brief period Shakespeare rises like a Jinn from a bottle till he seems to fill the sky. His early compositions, though written at an age older than the age at which Keats and Shelley had produced so much of their finest work, betray no signs of overwhelming power. The two long poems, composed when he was nearly thirty – that 'couple of ice-houses,' as Hazlitt called them, are pedantic studies of lust, without the least evidence of a dramatic gift – they are samples of good, sound, but uninspired Elizabethan verse. Yet two signs of power they do reveal: first of all that rich sensuousness and, indeed, sensuality which is almost a necessary part of great artistic endowment and with which no art, as Goethe said, can afford to dispense; – and with this, and due, no doubt, to a richness and concreteness of imagery and sense-impressions. A sensuous love of words they also show, and a meticulous care in the choice of phrases, a love of literary polish, and a laborious effort to acquire that mastery of language, which, to the artist whose medium of expression it is, must be the first and most essential endowment – or acquirement – of all.

II

There are two main methods of attaining excellence in writing, two ways of attempting to reach the peaks of Parnassus. The poet may attempt to fly thither on the wings of meaning, hoping that his high thoughts will float him aloft; or he may, step by step, cut his way thither with toil and labour. He may – to change the metaphor – begin by pressing out from life and experience the juice of meaning, and then find a receptacle to hold it; or the goldsmith's art may be his first preoccupation: he may carve and chisel and adorn his work with jewels, till at last the wine of imaginative meaning begins to fill the empty, elaborated cup. Shakespeare's early work shows that this latter method was his method. At the age of thirty he was still a euphuist, a lover of words for the sake of words, delighting in their sounds and rhymes and overtones, in 'taffeta phrases, silken terms precise', and, like Armado in his early play,

> One whom the music of his own vain tongue
> Doth ravish like enchanting harmony.

Of all that wealth of poetic emotion seeking to find expression, that mass of brooding thought we are aware of in the work of young poets like Shelley and Keats, there is no trace; we find at first in Shakespeare little more than a delight in verbal experiment and an unusual sensibility to the expressive and musical qualities of words.

Once, and once only in the history of a people, there comes a divine moment when its speech seems to those who write it a new-found wonder; when its language is in a plastic state, unstereotyped and unhackneyed; and it is at this moment that the one supreme poet, the Homer, the Dante, the Shakespeare, appears; for no form of speech seems rich enough to provide material for more than a single poet of this rank.

And what material as yet unexploited for literary purposes Shakespeare found ready at his hand! There were the learned vocabularies of the law and of theology, both of which he freely pillaged; there was the vigorous speech, full of wit and repartee and vituperation of the townsmen, innkeepers, shopkeepers, tradesmen of Stratford and of London; and beneath this the living talk of the countryside and the dialects of uplandish people, full of coarseness, and full also of the beautiful unconscious poetry of rustic speech, images and magical descriptive words and fresh country flowers with the breath of spring and the dew of the morning on them.

Shakespeare's plays, as Sir Walter Raleigh has said, are extraordinarily rich in the floating debris of popular proverbs, sayings, scraps and tags and broken ends of speech and song, caught out of the air or picked up by the roadside; and all this illiterate material he turned to the most exquisite literary use.

And then, in addition to these rich native sources, many wonderful new words were flooding into England from foreign lands; far-fetched, strange, exotic terms like *alligator, cannibal* and *hurricano*, and many others, brought home by English sailors and English pirates from the East and the West Indias, from Mexico and South America; and those aureate Italian words, imported into England by young Italianate travellers of fashion, words like *Paragon, Artist, Sonnet, Stanza, Madrigal, Conversation, Cavalier, Courtezan* and *Duello*.

III

But the passionate word-hunters of the time were not only collectors, but inventors as well. In addition to their generous hospitality, their willingness to welcome any of those terms 'of magnificence and splendour', which, as Dryden later said, must be imported from abroad, they were equally ready to experiment freely with native words, to try anything with them and see what happened, to make compounds of them, derivatives from them, to form verbs from nouns, and nouns from verbs and adjectives. In that age of complete linguistic freedom and experimental gusto the making of words became the sport of sports among the young intellectuals of fashion. How they created and coined and fantasticated them to please their fancy, made them ring and sing and rhyme together without a thought whether reason had any hand in the matter! In Shakespeare's early comedy, *Love's Labour's Lost*, we find, as Mr Gordon has said, the playground of the new language.

I know of no better description of the English of the time than that of Dr Abbott:

> for freedom, for brevity and for vigour, Elizabethan is superior to modern English. Many of the words employed by Shakespeare and his contemporaries were the recent inventions of the age; hence they were used with a freshness and exactness to which we are strangers. Again, the spoken English so far predominated over the grammatical English that it materially influenced the rhythm of the verse, the construction of the sentence, and even sometimes the spelling of words. Hence sprung an artless and unlaboured harmony which seems the natural heritage of Elizabethan poets, whereas such harmony as is attained by modern authors frequently betrays a painful excess of art. Lastly, the use of some few still remaining inflections (the subjunctive in particular), the lingering *sense* of many other inflections that had passed away leaving behind something of the old versatility and audacity in the arrangement of the sentence, the stern subordination of grammar to terseness and clearness, and the consequent directness and naturalness of expression, all conspire to give a liveliness and wakefulness to Shakespearian English which are wanting in the grammatical monotony of the present day. We may perhaps claim some superiority in completeness and perspicuity for modern English, but if we were to appeal on this ground to the shade of Shakespeare in the words of Antonio in the *Tempest*, –

> Do you not hear us speak?

we might fairly be crushed with the reply of Sebastian –

I do; and surely

It is a sleepy language.[1]

IV

Into this wild ocean of words Shakespeare plunged head over heels, and disported himself in it with a wild dolphin joy. He collected words from everywhere, from rustic speech and dialect (he no doubt spoke the Warwickshire dialect all his life), from Chaucer and old books, from translators of the classics, from lawyers and grave theologians, from travelled young gallants. He was, moreover, perhaps the greatest word-creator the world has ever known, and has probably added more new words to our vocabulary than all the other English poets put together. He made up his language as he went along – 'crashing', as he has been described, 'through the forest of words like a thunderbolt, crushing them out of shape if they don't fit in, melting moods and tenses, and leaving people to gape at the transformation.'

And yet he was by no means a word-eccentric like his contemporaries, Harvey and Chapman and Nashe, those magpies in their passion for odds and ends of language; he did not, like Spenser, make for himself a precious form of speech for his private use; he was no Anarch in this world of anarchy, but in the midst of the linguistic chaos of his time created a Paradise for the English-speaking race. His instinct for acceptable terms which might become current coin was unusually sure, and, as Mr Gordon says, his sensitiveness 'to the quality, the habits, and the history of the words he played with was a trained gift.' And Shakespeare possessed an even rarer gift, which can be best described by another quotation from Mr George Gordon's little masterpiece, *Shakespeare's English*,[2] his genius, namely, in the manipulation and development of meaning.

> It is exercised with habitual felicity on the commonest expressions in the language, and is an abstract of that shaping power exerted daily and almost unconsciously by every nation of speakers. The

miracle is to see so communal an engine in private hands. Shakespeare possessed this power in a degree never approached before or since by any Englishman, or perhaps by any individual mind; he seems, as he employs it, to be doing the work of a whole people.

Thus Shakespeare became, as I have said, the great Lord of Language, the most expressive, the most articulate of human beings.

What words or tongue of Seraph can suffice?

Raphael replied to Adam when our first parent asked that Archangel to recount the mighty record of God's creation of the world; and indeed, if ever there was a tongue which could suffice to tell of the wonders of this created world, that Seraph's tongue was Shakespeare's. He could say anything that could be said, describe both Nature and all its mighty works and clothe man's subtlest thoughts in the most transparent and luminous raiment of perfect expression.[3]

Shakespeare added, not only more words, but more figurative and proverbial phrases to our speech, than any other author has ever added to any language.[4] He may be regarded as being one of the great creators of the English language, and certainly it is owing to him that English, which till the end of the seventeenth century was almost unknown and never read abroad, has become a second speech to several other races; and it is hardly an exaggeration to say, as a Shakespeare enthusiast has said, that 'through his greatness a Low Dutch dialect has become the chiefest instrument of civilization, the world-speech of humanity at large.'[5]

V

And yet it is curious to note that the supremest gift of language, that gift of the magic and evocatory phrase, which has made Shakespeare the master-magician of the world, was by no means, with him, as with many young poets, a natural endowment; and we find few traces of it in the long poems he so carefully composed when nearly thirty. His

earliest plays are written in the common poetic diction of his time –
that style of the day which, as Swinburne says, all great poets begin by
writing, and lesser poets write all their lives. In the earlier historical
plays, where Shakespeare's authorship is disputed, it is hardly possible
to discriminate by any criterion of style which parts are of his
composition. In the powerful rhetoric and plangent declamation of
certain passages in these plays we seem to be first aware of
Shakespeare's gift of language; but it is only in the *Two Gentlemen of
Verona*, with the song 'Who is Silvia,' with the line:

> The uncertain glory of an April day,

and the passage about the brook that makes sweet music as it strays,
that his power over words becomes a magic power, and his golden
mastery of speech begins to almost blind us with its beauty.

Emerson describes how he once went to see the Hamlet of a famous
actor, and how all that he remembered of this great tragedian was
simply his question to the Ghost:

> What may this mean,
> That thou, dead corse, again in complete steel
> Revisit'st thus the glimpses of the moon?

This enchanted radiance of language, which for Emerson blotted out
the stage, the actor and the drama, is for some spectators or readers of
Shakespeare's plays the most potent spell which they cast upon him.
Of *Troilus and Cressida* they will remember the lines:

> I stalk about her door,
> Like a strange soul upon the Stygian banks
> Staying for waftage.

Or from *Timon*:

> Lie where the light foam of the sea may beat
> Thy grave-stone daily.

175

And even in that appalling play of beastly horror, *Titus Andronicus*, when the wretched Lavinia enters, 'ravished', according to the stage-directions, 'her hands cut off, and her tongue cut out', her uncle Marcus speaks of the villain who has mutilated her in a phrase 'by all the Muses filed':

> O! had the monster seen those lily hands
> Tremble, like aspen leaves, upon a lute!

It may also seem to such word-intoxicated readers as if Shakespeare sometimes used his plays merely for the opportunities they gave him for this lyric utterance; he turns the martial Othello and the savage Macbeth into supreme poets; he places, however incongruously, great verse in the mouth of any prosaic character who happens to be at hand, like Queen Gertrude's aria on Ophelia's death, or those lines of dark magic which he makes the thin lips of Iago utter:

> Not poppy, nor mandragora,
> Nor all the drowsy syrops of the world.

And what poetry he puts into the mouths of his murderers!

> Their lips were four red roses on a stalk,
> Which in their summer beauty kiss'd each other,

Forrest says, after his and Dighton's 'ruthless butchery' of the Princes in the Tower (*R. III*, IV, iii); and it is the first murderer in *Macbeth*, who, while they are waiting to slaughter Banquo, poetically remarks,

> The west yet glimmers with some streaks of day:
> Now spurs the lated traveller apace
> To gain the timely inn. (III, iii)

So too in enchanting words the savage Caliban describes the Enchanted Island to the drunken sailors:

Be not afeard: the isle is full of noises,
Sounds and sweet airs, that give delight, and hurt not.
Sometimes a thousand twanging instruments
Will hum about mine ears; and sometimes voices,
That, if I then had wak'd after long sleep,
Will make me sleep again: and then, in dreaming,
The clouds methought would open and show riches
Ready to drop upon me; that, when I wak'd,
I cried to dream again. (Tempest, III, ii)

Even on the granite face of the Professor in Minnesota we detect a smile; his lips, like the lips at sunrise of the great statue of Memnon, are touched with music as he speaks of the splendour of Shakespeare's poetry, 'shed' as he describes it 'like the rain and the light of heaven, on the just and the unjust.'

VI

This splendour of poetry – and Shakespeare, if not the most correct, is the most opulent and most magical of all poets – was the first of his genial gifts which reached maturity, and which in the *Two Gentlemen* and the plays of about that date makes its first shining appearance, flashes up, in *A Midsummer Night's Dream*, like a flood from an inexhaustible fountain. Of the great poetry in the other great lyrical plays of this period, in *Romeo and Juliet*, in the *Merchant of Venice*, and in *Richard II*, and in the three Golden Comedies which followed, I need not speak; this middle style of Shakespeare's poetry, could it be imitated, would be the most perfect model and absolute pattern of what poetry should be. But it cannot be imitated: unlike Æschylus or Virgil or Dante or Milton, Shakespeare has no mannerisms: we recognize his lines only by their supreme felicity, their 'effortless power', as it has been well described, 'and their incomparable sweetness.'

And yet there is one quality or characteristic of Shakespeare's poetry which, though it cannot be imitated, distinguishes it from that of all other poets. This quality is his possession, in a supreme degree, of the

177

greatest of all poetic gifts, a sensuous, pictorial imagination, and the power of embodying his thoughts in images of beauty and splendour. 'Every word,' as Gray said of him, 'is a picture'; and these pictures often flash from the length of a line or phrase with the quickness of lightning-flashes. This unparalleled wealth of imagery shows itself, above all, in that royal use of metaphor, which is the most distinguishing quality of his style, and which Aristotle described, as the surest mark of genius. 'He could not speak but a figure came.' His thought passes from metaphor to metaphor, each of them bringing a glint of colour and suggestion, and forming an iridescent, or a dark and shadowy, background to the scenes depicted. These metaphors he draws from every source, from trees, from flowers, from the sea and clouds, and seasons, and from the simplest, humblest things of the house or farm, from domestic animals, cats and dogs, or from the nobler creatures of the wild, from eagles, deer and lions or fierce tigers, and above all from the features and movements of the human body. He even brings to life the half-obliterated images of popular idiom, each with a figure or action, a shade of feeling of its own, which, as Maeterlinck pointed out, no translator is able to translate to another language.

Shakespeare does not confine himself, like many poets, only to visual images; he makes use of impressions from the other senses, the senses of smell and hearing; and seems to have been especially fond of images of reverberating sound, trumpets and horns and the baying of hounds echoing from afar. Motor images as they are called, sensations of effort, strain, movement, of rushing winds or horses, are frequent in his poetry, and also of the tides and the surges of the sea ('surge' is a favourite word with Shakespeare) and of the flow of rivers, as in one of his most splendid images, of the Pontic sea:

> Whose icy current and compulsive course
> Ne'er feels retiring ebb, but keeps due on
> To the Propontic and the Hellespont.

VII

Shakespeare uses his images, his similes and metaphors, at first in the manner of Spenser and most other poets, as decorations and adornments of his verse. When, for instance, Romeo, in his early play, sees Juliet at the window and exclaims:

> It is the east, and Juliet is the sun!
> Arise, fair sun, and kill the envious moon,
> Who is already sick and pale with grief.

These images, and those that follow about the moon's vestal livery and Juliet's eyes twinkling like stars in heaven, are pure decoration, and very pretty and conceited decoration they make. But as Shakespeare grows in poetic power, he employs his images, not only for ornament, but for far higher purposes; his metaphors, transmuted in his imagination, interpret and in a sense create the life he depicts. Of this kind of creative imagery he becomes with Æschylus a supreme master. If we read again the familiar passage in *Macbeth*:

> To-morrow, and to-morrow, and to-morrow,
> Creeps in this petty pace from day to day,
> To the last syllable of recorded time;
> And all our yesterdays have lighted fools
> The way to dusty death. Out, out, brief candle!
> Life's but a walking shadow, a poor player
> That struts and frets his hour upon the stage,
> And then is heard no more; it is a tale
> Told by an idiot, full of sound and fury,
> Signifying nothing,

we cannot but see how such images in this supremely imaginative passage, whether visual, – 'lighted', and 'brief candle'; or audible, – 'syllable', 'heard no more', 'sound and fury'; – or the motor images, – 'creeps', 'walking shadow', 'struts and frets' – are no mere decorations; and in general we may say that the great Shakespearean characters, like primitive man, create what they express by clothing their ideas in images.

VIII

But Shakespeare uses his metaphors in a still more subtle and sublime fashion. Maeterlinck, in his Preface to his translation of *Macbeth*, notes how the deep impression which this play makes upon us is due to the images which swarm in the speeches of the characters, who thus make the atmosphere they breathe, and who become in turn the tragic creatures of that atmosphere. It is the innumerable stir and whisper of these images, he says, which give its inner and profound life to *Macbeth*; and though we are hardly conscious of them, they are the cause of the inexplicable power of the play upon us.

This special tone or atmosphere in *Macbeth* is described by Dr Bradley as being due, in part at least, to the frequent occurrence of images of darkness and night, or rather of black night broken by flashes of light and colour; and that colour was especially the colour of blood.[6]

Blood, Blood, Blood! these dreadful images, these awful metaphors, keep muttering 'Blood' in a kind of undersong all through the play. Macbeth sees gouts of blood on the imaginary dagger before Duncan's murder; blood on his own hands afterwards, blood that not all the green ocean could wash away, but would rather stain the multitudinous sea with red; he invokes the 'bloody and invisible' hand of night before Banquo's murder; 'there's blood upon thy face;' he whispers to the murderer at the banquet afterwards, and says, 'Never shake thy gory locks at me!' to the ghost of Banquo.

It will have blood, they say; blood will have blood,

he cries, when the guests have departed; and in the cavern scene, where the apparition of 'a bloody child' bids him 'be bloody, bold, and resolute', still the blood-boltered Banquo smiles in awful derision upon him.

Lady Macbeth too is haunted by images of blood; cannot wash the smell of it from her hand; while Malcolm and Macduff in England lament the bleeding of their country under the 'bloody-scepter'd tyrant'; and Lennox prays for feasts and banquets freed from 'bloody knives'; and as Macbeth's enemies approach Dunsinane, one of them describes his deeds in what is perhaps the most terrible metaphor of the play; terrible, because blood is suggested by its texture, but is not named:

> Now does he feel
> His secret murders sticking on his hands.

I quote from Dr Caroline Spurgeon, who has carried much further the suggestion of the reiteration of images in Shakespeare's plays, her hypothesis being that not only *Macbeth*, but each of the great tragedies has a dominating image, or set of images, which, like a floating picture, or under-song of recurrent themes and *motivs* in music, gives to each its special tone, atmosphere and colour. The tragedy of *Romeo and Juliet*, for instance, is full of images of light, the flash of brilliant light quenched suddenly in darkness. Out of candlelight, torches, the sparkle of fire, the flash of power, and especially of bright or evil stars, Shakespeare forms, for the story of these 'star-crossed' lovers, and their love – too quick, too quickly quenched – 'too like the lightning', as Juliet herself describes it, or in the Friar's words:

> Like fire and powder,
> Which as they kiss consume –

out of these he forms, Dr Spurgeon writes, 'a continuous and consistent running image of exquisite beauty, building up a definite picture and atmosphere of brilliance swiftly quenched, which powerfully affects the imagination of the reader.'

The dominating metaphors in *Hamlet*, she says, are images of illness and disease, of some tumour, a hidden rank corruption, which, 'mining all within, infects unseen.'

The atmosphere of space and magnitude which surrounds the figures in *Antony and Cleopatra* is created, she adds, by recurring images of great elemental forces, of the wide world, of the sun and moon and the sea and sky and vastness generally; of that 'demi-Atlas of the earth', Antony, who was willing to let, for Cleopatra's love, 'the wide arch of the ranged empire' fall; so that, when this giant fell himself, his paramour could find

> Nothing left remarkable
> Beneath the visiting moon.[7]

It was, however, not these great qualities that charmed Shakespeare's contemporaries, but the 'honey-tongued sweetness' of his wood-notes wild; this is the quality of his verse they always notice; and surely for us, at least this blackbird's fluting, and the divine airs which he, like Mozart, seems to have caught from heaven, can never lose, any more than the blackbird's song or Mozart's music can lose, their enchantment, even in our disenchanted ears.

The Merchant of Venice is not for many lovers of Shakespeare one of their favourite plays. Its theatricality and stage-effectiveness put a cheat upon them which they afterwards resent. But the other day, when I happened to look into it – 'The Moon shines bright' – these first words of the last Act beguiled me with their magic:

> In such a night as this,
> When the sweet wind did gently kiss the trees
> And they did make no noise –
> In such a night
> Stood Dido with a willow in her hand
> Upon the wild sea banks, and waft her love
> To come again to Carthage, –

when Lorenzo and Jessica were out-nighting each other in such a night as this, what could I do but revel in the moonlight and enchanted echoes of this scene?

> Sit, Jessica: look, how the floor of heaven
> Is thick inlaid with patines of bright gold:
> There's not the smallest orb which thou behold'st
> But in his motion like an angel sings,
> Still quiring to the young-eyed cherubins:
> Such harmony is in immortal souls;

> But, whilst this muddy vesture of decay
> Doth grossly close it in, we cannot hear it.

Poetry was given to man, Goethe said, to make him satisfied with himself and with his lot. Certainly for me poetry, either in verse or prose, exquisitely performs this function. I may be old and cross and ill, a wasted life may lie behind me, and the grave yawn close in front. I may have lost my faith, my illusions and hopes, my reputation and umbrella. What does it matter? It doesn't matter in the least! Reading Lorenzo's words,

> Come, ho! and wake Diana with a hymn!

off I go into the enchanted forest, into the Age of Gold. Life ceases to be brief, sad, enigmatic; I am perfectly satisfied with it. What more is there indeed to ask for? I taste a joy beyond the reach of fate; *le bonheur, l'impossible bonheur*, is mine. I am (to express myself in soberer terms) simply kidnapped into heaven. I sit with the Gods and quaff their nectar; quaff indeed a nectar more generous than their own, since I, alone of the Immortals, taste the aroma of this aromatic, floating, orchard plot of earth, which, could they but sip its fragrance, how gladly would the Gods descend from their golden chairs, take upon themselves the burden of our earthly sin, and provoke another Flood! Even that 'fading mansion', my aching, coughing body, becomes a vehicle and instrument of music, and, like a battered old violin, shivers and vibrates with tunable delight. 'Therefore the poet,' as Lorenzo went on to tell Jessica,

> Did feign that Orpheus drew trees, stones, and flood;
> Since naught so stockish, hard, and full of rage,
> But music for the time doth change his nature.

If ever again I am so stockish or full of rage as to deny the genius of Shakespeare, the music of this scene will, in the magical five minutes it takes to read it through, charm me back from my backsliding.

By the time he had written *Hamlet* it would seem as if Shakespeare had reached perfection as a poet: as if the mastery of the art of language could be carried no further point. But as we watch the onrush of his genius, one of the things which almost take our breath is the way he will leap beyond what seems perfection to heights above anything we could have possibly imagined. After *Hamlet*, the sweet perfection of his verse is more and more replaced by a more vehement and vaster music, and by passages illuminated, as by flashes of lightning, with phrases of supreme simplicity, but of supreme sublimity, in which the meaning is no longer set, as it were, to the music and patterned to the rhythm of his verse, but creates its own rhythm and is the very essence of that rhythm — a few words which, transcending all rhetoric and poetry, illuminate the darkness of some tragic situation and carry with them an unequalled sense of strangeness and an almost intolerable poignancy.

> It is the cause, it is the cause, my soul —
> Tomorrow, and tomorrow, and tomorrow —
> > The long day's task is done,
> And we must sleep.
> > My heart dances;
> But not for joy; not joy —
> No, no, no life! —
> > Thou'lt come no more,
> Never, never, never, never, never!

There are poets, it may be, who have written poetry as great, or nearly as great as that of Shakespeare, but no poet has ever approached sublimity like this; this beauty beyond beauty belongs to him alone — in the circle of that great magic none dare walk but he.

1. A *Shakespearian Grammar*, E. A. Abbott (Macmillan).
2. *S.P.E. Tract, No. XXIX*, Oxford Press, 1928.
3. 'There has never been a writer,' as Sir Walter Raleigh says, 'who came nearer to giving adequate verbal expression to the subtlest turns of consciousness, the flitting shadows and half-conceived ideas and purposes which count for so much in the life of the mind.' (*Shakespeare*, p. 216.)

4. I give a list of about one hundred of these in my *Words and Idioms*, pp. 227–228.
5. *The Man Shakespeare*, Frank Harris, p. xix.
6. *Shakespearean Tragedy*, p. 335.
7. Dr Spurgeon has made a prolonged study of Shakespeare's images, the results of which she promises to give before long to the world. So far she has published only two fascinating but most tantalizing foretastes of the feast she promises; a pamphlet (from which I have quoted above) of the Shakespeare Association entitled, *Leading Motives in the Imagery of Shakespeare's Tragedies* (Oxford Press, 1930), and *Shakespeare's Iterative Imagery*, British Academy Lecture, 1931 (Oxford Press).

PART III: FICTIONS

1. from

Trivia (1918)

FROM BOOK I

—— ✳ ——

Preface

'You must beware of thinking too much about Style,' said my kindly adviser, 'or you will become like those fastidious people who polish and polish until there is nothing left.'

'Then there really are such people?' I asked eagerly. But the well-informed lady could give me no precise information about them.

I often hear of them in this tantalizing manner, and perhaps one of these days I shall have the luck to come across them.

Happiness

Cricketers on village greens, hay-makers in the evening sunshine, small boats that sail before the wind – all these create in me the illusion of Happiness, as if a land of cloudless pleasure, a piece of the old Golden World, were hidden, not (as poets have fancied) in far seas or beyond inaccessible mountains, but here close at hand, if one could find it, in some undiscovered valley. Certain grassy lanes seem to lead through the copses thither; the wild pigeons talk of it behind the woods.

The wheat

The Vicar, whom I met once or twice in my walks about the fields, told me that he was glad that I was taking an interest in farming. Only my feeling about wheat, he said, puzzled him.

Now the feeling in regard to wheat which I had not been able to make clear to the Vicar, was simply one of amazement. Walking one day into a field that I had watched yellowing beyond the trees, I was dazzled by the glow and great expanse of gold. I bathed myself in the intense yellow under the intense blue sky; how it dimmed the oak trees and copses and all the rest of the English landscape! I had not remembered the glory of the Wheat; nor imagined in my reading that in a country so far from the Sun, there could be anything so rich, so prodigal, so reckless, as this opulence of ruddy gold, bursting out from the cracked earth as from some fiery vein beneath. I remembered how for thousands of years Wheat had been the staple of wealth, the hoarded wealth of famous cities and empires; I thought of the processes of corn-growing, the white oxen ploughing, the great barns, the winnowing fans, the mills with the splash of their wheels, or arms slow-turning in the wind; of cornfields at harvest-time, with shocks and sheaves in the glow of sunset, or under the sickle moon; what beauty it brought into the northern landscape, the antique, passionate, Biblical beauty of the South!

In church

'For the Pen,' said the Vicar; and in the sententious pause which followed I felt that I would offer any gifts of gold to avert or postpone the solemn, inevitable, and yet, as it seemed to me, perfectly appalling statement that 'the Pen is mightier than the Sword.'

Parsons

All the same I like Parsons; they think nobly of the Universe, and believe in Souls and Eternal Happiness. And some of them, I am told, believe in Angels – that there are Angels who guide our footsteps, and flit to and fro unseen on errands in the air about us.

High life

Although that immense Country House was empty and for sale, and I had got an order to view it, I needed all my courage to walk through the lordly gates, and up the avenue, and then to ring the door-bell. And when I was ushered in, and the shutters were removed to let the daylight into those vast apartments, I sneaked through them, cursing the dishonest curiosity which had brought me into a place where I had no business. But I was treated with such deference, and so plainly regarded as a possible purchaser, that I soon began to believe in the opulence imputed to me. From all the novels describing the mysterious and glittering life of the Great which I had read (and I have read thousands), there came to me the vision of my own existence in this Palace. I filled those vast halls with the shine of jewels and stir of voices; I saw a vision of ladies sweeping in their tiaras down the splendid stairs.

But my Soul, in her swell of pride, soon outgrew these paltry limits. Oh no! Never could I box up and house under that roof the Pomp, the Ostentation of which I was capable.

Then for one thing there was stabling for only forty horses; and this, of course, as I told them, would never do.

At the window

But then I drew up the curtain and looked out of the window. Yes, there it still was, the old External World, still apparently quite unaware of its own non-existence. I felt helpless, small-boyish before it: I couldn't pooh-pooh it away.

They

Their taste is exquisite; They live in Palladian houses, in a world of ivory and precious china, of old brickwork and stone pilasters. In white drawing-rooms I see Them, or on blue, bird-haunted lawns. They talked pleasantly of me, and Their eyes watch me. From the diminished, ridiculous picture of myself which the glass of the world gives me, I turn for comfort, for happiness to my image in the kindly mirror of those eyes.

Who are they? Where, in what paradise or palace, shall I ever find Them? I may walk all the streets, ring all the door-bells of the World, but I shall never find Them. Yet nothing has value for me save in the crown of Their approval; for Their coming – which will never be – I build and plant, and for Them alone I secretly write this Book, which They will never read.

Caravans

Always over the horizon of the Sahara move those soundless caravans of camels, swaying with their padded feet across the desert, till in the remoteness of my mind they fade away, and vanish.

The full moon

And then one night, low above the trees, we saw the great, amorous, unabashed face of the full Moon. It was an exhibition that made me blush, feel that I had no right to be there. 'After all these millions of years, she ought to be ashamed of herself !' I cried.

The snob

As I paced in fine company on that terrace, I felt chosen, exempt, and curiously happy. There was a glamour in the air, a something in the special flavour of that moment that was like the consciousness of Salvation, or the smell of ripe peaches on a sunny wall.

I know what you're going to call me, Reader; but I am not to be bullied by words. And, after all, why not let oneself be dazzled and enchanted? Are not illusions pleasant, and is this a world in which Romance hangs, so to speak, on every tree?

And how about your own life? Is that, then, so full of golden visions?

The rose

The old lady had always been proud of the great rose-tree in her garden, and was fond of telling how it had grown from a cutting she had brought years before from Italy, when she was first married. She and her husband had been travelling back in their carriage from Naples (it was before the time of railways), and on a bad piece of road south of Sienna they had broken down, and had been forced to pass the night in a little house by the roadside. The accommodation was wretched of course; she had spent a sleepless night, and rising early had stood, wrapped up, at her window, with the cool air blowing on her face, to watch the dawn. She could still, after all these years, remember the blue mountains with the bright moon above them, and how a far-off town on one of the peaks had gradually grown whiter and whiter, till the moon faded, the mountains were touched with the pink of the rising sun, and suddenly the town was lit as by an illumination, one window after another catching and reflecting the sun's beams, till at last the whole little city twinkled and sparkled up in the sky like a nest of stars.

Finding they would have to wait while their carriage was being repaired, they had driven that morning, in a local conveyance, up to the city on the mountain, where they had been told they would find better quarters; and there they had stayed two or three days. It was one of the miniature Italian cities with a high church, a pretentious piazza, a few narrow streets and little palaces, perched, all compact and complete, on the top of a mountain, within an enclosure of walls hardly larger than an English kitchen garden. But it was full of life and noise, echoing all day and all night with the sounds of feet and voices.

The Café of the simple inn where they stayed was the meeting-place of the notabilities of the little city; the *Sindaco*, the *avvocato*, the doctor, and a few others; and among them they noticed a beautiful, slim, talkative old man, with bright black eyes and snow-white hair – tall and straight and still with the figure of a youth, although the waiter told them with pride that the *Conte* was *molto vecchio* – would in fact be eighty in the following year. He was the last of his family, the waiter added – they had once been great and rich people – but he had no descendants; in fact the waiter mentioned with complacency, as if it were a story on which the locality prided itself, that the *Conte* had been unfortunate in love, and had never married.

The old gentleman, however, seemed cheerful enough; and it was plain that he took an interest in the strangers, and wished to make their acquaintance. This was soon effected by the friendly waiter; and after a little talk the old man invited them to visit his villa and garden which were just outside the walls of the town. So the next afternoon, when the sun began to descend, and they saw in glimpses through doorways and windows blue shadows spreading over the brown mountains, they went to pay their visit. It was not much of a place, a small, modernized, stucco villa, with a hot pebbly garden, and in it a stone basin with torpid gold fish, and a statue of Diana and her hounds against the wall. But what gave a glory to it was a gigantic rose-tree which clambered over the house, almost smothering the windows, and filling the air with the perfume of its sweetness. Yes, it was a fine rose, the *Conte* said proudly when they praised it, and he would tell the Signora about it. And as they sat there, drinking the wine he offered them, he alluded with the cheerful indifference of old age to his love affair, as though he took for granted that they had heard of it already.

'The lady lived across the valley there beyond that hill. I was a young man then, for it was many years ago. I used to ride over to see her; it was a long way, but I rode fast, for young men, as no doubt the Signora knows, are impatient. But the lady was not kind, she would keep me waiting, oh, for hours; and one day when I had waited very long I grew very angry, and as I walked up and down in the garden where she had told me she would see me, I broke one of her roses, broke a branch from it; and when I saw what I had done, I hid it inside my coat – so –; and when I came home I planted it, and the Signora sees how it has grown. If the Signora admires it, I must give her a cutting to plant also

194

in her garden; I am told the English have beautiful gardens that are green, and not burnt with the sun like ours.'

The next day, when their mended carriage had come up to fetch them, and they were just starting to drive away from the inn, the *Conte*'s old servant appeared with the rose-cutting neatly wrapped up, and the compliments and wishes for a *buon viaggio* from her master. The town collected to see them depart, and the children ran after their carriage through the gate of the little city. They heard a rush of feet behind them for a few moments, but soon they were far down toward the valley; the little town with all its noise and life was high above them on its mountain peak.

She had planted the rose at home, where it had grown and flourished in a wonderful manner; and every June the great mass of leaves and shoots still broke out into a passionate splendour of scent and crimson colour, as if in its root and fibres there still burnt the anger and thwarted desire of that Italian lover. Of course, said the old lady (who had outlived sixty generations of these roses), the old *Conte* must have died long ago; she had forgotten his name, and had even forgotten the name of the mountain city that she had stayed in, after first seeing it twinkling at dawn in the sky, like a nest of stars.

The spider

What shall I compare it to, this fantastic thing I call my Mind? To a waste-paper basket, to a sieve choked with sediment, or to a barrel full of floating froth and refuse?

No, what it is really most like is a spider's web, insecurely hung on leaves and twigs, quivering in every wind, and sprinkled with dew-drops and dead flies. And at its geometric centre, pondering for ever the Problem of Existence, sits motionless and spiderlike the uncanny Soul.

FROM BOOK II

———— ✻ ————

At the bank

Entering the Bank in a composed manner, I drew a cheque and handed it to the cashier through the grating. Then I eyed him narrowly. Would not that astute official see that I was posing as a Real Person? No; he calmly opened a little drawer, took out some real sovereigns, counted them carefully, and handed them to me in a brass shovel. I went away feeling I had perpetrated a delightful fraud. I had got some of the gold of the actual world!

Yet now and then, at the sight of my name on a visiting card, or of my face photographed in a group among other faces, or when I see a letter addressed in my hand, or catch the sound of my own voice, I grow shy in the presence of a mysterious Person who is myself, is known by my name, and who apparently does exist. Can it be possible that I am as real as any one, and that all of us – the cashier and banker at the Bank, the King on his throne – all feel ourselves ghosts and goblins in this authentic world?

Appearance and reality

It is pleasant to saunter out in the morning sun and idle along the summer streets with no purpose.

But is it Right?

I am not really bothered by these Questions – the hoary old puzzles of Ethics and Philosophy, which lurk around the London corners to waylay me. I have got used to them; and the most formidable of all, the biggest bug of Metaphysics, the Problem which nonplusses the wisest heads on this Planet, has become quite a familiar companion of mine.

What is Reality? I ask myself almost daily: how does the External World exist, materialized in mid-air, apart from my perceptions? This show of streets and skies, of policemen and perambulators and hard pavements, is it nothing more than a mere hypothesis and figment of the Mind, or does it remain there, permanent and imposing, when I stop looking at it?

Often, as I saunter along Piccadilly or Bond Street, I please myself with the Berkeleian notion that Matter has no existence, that this so solid-seeming World is all idea, all appearance – that I am carried soft through space inside an immense Thought-bubble, a floating, diaphanous, opaltinted Dream.

I see the world

'But you go nowhere, see nothing of the world,' my cousins said.

Now though I do go sometimes to the parties to which I am now and then invited, I find, as a matter of fact, that I get really much more pleasure by looking in at windows, and have a way of my own of seeing the World. And of summer evenings, when motors hurry through the late twilight, and the great houses take on airs of inscrutable expectation, I go owling out through the dusk; and wandering toward the West, lose my way in unknown streets – an unknown City of revels. And when a door opens and a bediamonded Lady moves to her motor over carpets unrolled by powdered footmen, I can easily think her some great Courtezan, or some half-believed-in Duchess, hurrying to card-tables and candelabra and strange scenes of joy. I like to see that there are still splendid people on this flat earth; and at dances, standing in the street with the crowd, and stirred by the music, the lights, the rushing sound of voices, I think the Ladies as beautiful as Stars who move up lanes of light into those Palaces; the young men look like Lords in novels; and if (it has once or twice happened) people I know go by me, they strike me as changed and rapt beyond my sphere. And when on hot nights windows are left open, and I can look in at Dinner Parties, as I peer through lace curtains and window-flowers at the silver, the women's shoulders, the shimmer of their jewels, and the divine attitudes of their heads as they lean and listen, I imagine extraordinary intrigues and unheard-of wines and passions.

Longevity

'But when you are as old as I am!' I said to the young lady in pink satin.

'But I don't know how old you are,' the young lady in pink answered almost archly. We were getting on quite nicely.

'Oh, I'm endlessly old; my memory goes back almost for ever. I come out of the Middle Ages. I am the primitive savage we are all descended from; I believe in Devil-worship and the power of the Stars; I dance under the new Moon, naked and tattooed and holy. I am a Cavedweller, a contemporary of Mastodons and Mammoths; I am pleistocene and eolithic, and full of the lusts and terrors of the great pre-glacial forests. But that's nothing; I am millions of years older; I am an arboreal Ape, an aged Baboon, with all its instincts; I am a pre-simian quadruped, I have great claws, eyes that see in the dark, and a long prehensile tail.'

'Good gracious!' said the terrified young lady in pink satin. Then she turned and talked in a hushed voice with her other neighbour.

In the bus

As I sat inside that crowded bus, so sad, so incredible and sordid seemed the fat face of the woman opposite me, that I interposed the thought of Kilimanjaro, that highest mountain of Africa, between us; the grassy slopes and green Arcadian realms of negro kings from which its dark cone rises; the immense, dim, elephant-haunted forests which clothe its flanks, and above, the white crown of snow, freezing in eternal isolation over the palm trees and deserts of the African Equator.

199

The saying of a Persian poet

All this hurry to dress and go out, these journeys in taxicabs, or in trains with my packed bag from big railway stations – what keeps me going, I sometimes ask myself; and I remember how, in his 'Masnavi I Ma'navi' or 'Spiritual Couplets', Jalalu 'D-Din Muhammad Rumi tells us that the swarm of gaudy Thoughts we pursue and follow are short-lived like summer insects, and must all be killed before long by the winter of age.

'Where do I come in?'

When I read in the *Times* about India and all its problems and populations; when I look at the letters in large type of important personages, and find myself face to face with the Questions, Movements, and great Activities of the Age, 'Where do I come in?' I ask uneasily.

Then in the great *Times*-reflected world I find the corner where I play my humble but necessary part. For I am one of the unpraised, unrewarded millions without whom Statistics would be a bankrupt science. It is we who are born, who marry, who die, in constant ratios; who regularly lose so many umbrellas, post just so many unaddressed letters every year. And there are enthusiasts among us, Heroes who, without the least thought of their own convenience, allow omnibuses to run over them, or throw themselves month by month, in fixed numbers, from the London bridges.

The power of words

I thanked the club porter who helped me into my coat, and stepped out gayly into the vastness of the Night. And as I walked along my eyes were dazzling with the glare behind me; I heard the sound of my speech, the applause and laughter.

And when I looked up at the Stars, the great Stars that bore me company, streaming over the dark houses as I moved, I felt that I was the Lord of Life; the mystery and disquieting meaninglessness of existence – the existence of other people, and of my own, were solved for me now. As for the Earth, hurrying beneath my feet, how bright was its journey; how shining the goal toward which it went swinging – you might really say leaping – through the sky.

'I must tell the Human Race of this!' I heard my voice; saw my prophetic gestures, as I expounded the ultimate meaning of existence to the white, rapt faces of Humanity. Only to find the words – that troubled me; were there then no words to describe this Vision – divine – intoxicating?

And then the Word struck me; the Word people would use. I stopped in the street; my Soul was silenced like a bell that snarls at a jarring touch. I stood there awhile and meditated on language, its perfidious meanness, the inadequacy, the ignominy of our vocabulary, and how Moralists have spoiled our words by distilling into them, as into little vials of poison, all their hatred of human joy.

Away with that police-trial of brutal words which bursts in on our best moments and arrests our finest feelings! This music within me, large, like the song of the stars – like a Glory of Angels singing, – 'No one has any right to say I am drunk!' I shouted.

The incredible

'Yes, but they were afraid of you.'

'Afraid of *me*?'

'Yes, so one of them told me afterwards.'

I was fairly jiggered. If my personality can inspire fear or respect, the world must be a simpler place than I had thought it. Afraid of a twittering shadow, a make-believe like me? Are children more absurdly terrified by a candle in a hollow turnip? Was Bedlam at full moon ever scared by anything half so silly?

The poplar

There is a great tree in Sussex, whose cloud of thin foliage floats high in the summer air. The thrush sings in that umbrage, and blackbirds, who fill the late, decorative sunshine with a shimmer of golden sound. There the nightingale finds her green cloister; and on those branches sometimes, like a great fruit, hangs the lemon-coloured Moon. In the glare of August, when all the world is faint with heat, there is always a breeze in those cool recesses; always a noise, like the noise of water, among their lightly-hung leaves.

But the owner of this Tree lives in London, reading books.

Under an umbrella

From under the roof of my umbrella I saw the washed pavement lapsing beneath my feet, the news-posters lying smeared with dirt at the crossings, the tracks of the buses in the liquid mud. On I went through this world of wetness. And through what long perspectives of the years shall I still hurry down wet streets – middle-aged, and then, perhaps, very old? And on what errands?

Asking myself this question I fade from your vision, Reader, into the distance, sloping my umbrella against the wind.

2. from

More Trivia (1922)

Reassurance

I look at my overcoat and my hat hanging in the hall with reassurance; for although I go out of doors with one individuality today, when yesterday I had quite another, yet my clothes keep my various selves buttoned up together, and enable all these otherwise irreconcilable aggregates of psychological phenomena to pass themselves off as one person.

The great adventure

I paused, before opening the front-door, for a moment of deep consideration.

Dim-lit, shadowy, full of menace and unimaginable chances, stretched all around my door the many-peopled streets. I could hear ominous and muffled, the tides of multitudinous traffic, sounding along their ways. Was I equipped for the navigation of those waters, armed and ready to adventure out into that dangerous world again?

Gloves? Money? Cigarettes? Matches? Yes; and I had an umbrella for its tempests, and a latchkey for my safe return.

The ghost

When people talk of Ghosts I don't mention the Apparition by which I am haunted, the Phantom that shadows me about the streets, the image or spectre, so familiar, so like myself, which lurks in the plate-glass of shop-windows, or leaps out of mirrors to waylay me.

The suburbs

What are the beliefs about God in Grosvenor Gardens, the surmises of South Kensington concerning our fate beyond the Grave? On what ground does life seem worth living in Pimlico; and how far in the Cromwell Road do they follow, or think they follow, the precepts of the Sermon on the Mount?

If I can but dimly discern the ideals of these familiar regions, how much more am I in the dark about the inner life of the great outer suburbs. In what works of local introspection can I study the day-dreams of Hoxton, the curiosities and discouragements of Clapham or Ealing?

More than once I have paused before a suburban villa, telling myself that I had after all but to ring the bell, and go in and ask them. But alas, they would not tell me; they could not tell me, even if they would.

Good practice

We met in an omnibus last evening. 'And where are you going now?' she asked, as she looked at me with amusement.

'I am going, if the awful truth must be told, to dine in Grosvenor Square.'

'Lord!' she colloquially replied, 'and what do you do that for?'

'I do it because I am invited. And besides,' I went on, 'let me remind you of what the Persian Mystics say of the Saints – that the Saints are sometimes rich, that God sometimes endows Those Holy Ones with an outward show of wealth to hide them from the profane.'

'Oh, does He? – Hides them in Grosvenor Square?'

'Very well then, I shall tell you the real truth; I shall tell you my real reason for going to dine there. Do you remember what Diogenes replied when they wanted to know why he had asked for a statue to be erected at the public expense in his honour?'

'No; what did he say?'

'He said – but I must explain another time. I have to get off here. Good-night.'

I paused, however, at the door of the bus. 'He said,' I called back, 'I am practising Disappointment.'

Evasion

'And what do you think of the International Situation?' asked that foreign Countess, with her foreign, fascinating smile.

Was she a Spy? I felt I must be careful.

'What do I think?' I evasively echoed; and then, carried away by the profound and melancholy interest of this question, 'Think?' I queried, 'do I ever really think? Is there anything inside my head but cotton-wool? How can I, with a mind full of grey monkeys with blue faces, call myself a Thinker? What am I anyhow?' I pursued the sad inquiry: 'A noodle, a pigwidgeon, a ninny-hammer – a bubble on the wave, Madame, a leaf in the wind!'

Sir Eustace Carr

When I read the news about Sir Eustace Carr in the morning paper, I was startled, like everyone else who knew, if only by name, this young man, whose wealth and good looks, whose adventurous travels and whose brilliant and happy marriage, had made of him an almost romantic figure.

Every now and then one hears of some strange happening of this kind. But they are acts so anomalous, in such startling contradiction to all our usual ways and accepted notions of life and its value, that most of us are willing enough to accept the familiar explanation of insanity, or any other commonplace cause which may be alleged – financial trouble, or some passionate entanglement, and the fear of scandal and exposure. And then the Suicide is forgotten as soon as possible, and his memory shuffled out of the way as something unpleasant to think of. But I sometimes wonder about these cases, asking myself whether the dead man may not have carried to the grave with him the secret of some strange perplexity, some passion or craving or irresistible impulse, of which perhaps his intimates, and certainly the coroner's jury, can have had no inkling.

I had never met or spoken to Sir Eustace Carr – the worlds we lived in were very different – but I had read of his explorations in the East, and of the curious tombs he had discovered – somewhere, was it not? – in the Nile Valley. Then, too, it happened (and this was the main cause of my interest) that at one time I had seen him more than once, under circumstances that were rather unusual. And now I began to think of this incident. In a way it was nothing, and yet the impression haunted me that it was somehow connected with this final act, for which no explanation, beyond that of sudden mental derangement, had been offered. This explanation did not seem to me wholly adequate, although it had been accepted, I believe, both by his friends and the general public – and with the more apparent reason on account of a strain of eccentricity, amounting in some cases almost to insanity which could be traced, it was said, in his mother's family.

I found it not difficult to revive with a certain vividness the memory of those cold and rainy November weeks that I had happened to spend alone, some years ago, in Venice, and of the churches which I had so frequently haunted. Especially I remembered the great dreary church in the *campo* near my lodgings, into which I would often go on my way to my rooms in the twilight. It was the season when all the Venice churches are draped in black, and services for the dead are held in them at dawn and twilight; and when I entered this Baroque interior, with its twisted columns and volutes and high-piled, hideous tombs, adorned with skeletons and allegorical figures and angels blowing trumpets – all so agitated, and yet all so dead and empty and frigid – I would find the fantastic darkness filled with glimmering candles, and kneeling figures, and the discordant noise of chanting. There I would sit, while outside night fell with the rain on Venice; the palaces and green canals faded into darkness, and the great bells, swinging against the low sky, sent the melancholy sound of their voices far over the lagoons.

It was here, in this church, that I used to see Sir Eustace Carr; would generally find him in the same corner when I entered, and would sometimes watch his face, until the ceremonious extinguishing of the candles, one by one, left us in shadowy night. It was a handsome and thoughtful face, and I remember more than once wondering what had brought him to Venice in that unseasonable month, and why he came so regularly to this monotonous service. It was as if some spell had drawn him; and now, with my curiosity newly wakened, I asked myself what had been that spell? I also must have been affected by it, for I had been there also in his uncommunicating company. Here, I felt, was perhaps the answer to my question, the secret of the enigma that puzzled me; and as I went over my memories of that time, and revived its sombre and almost sinister fascination, I seemed to see an answer looming before my imagination. But it was an answer, an hypothesis or supposition, so fantastic, that my common sense could hardly accept it. For I now saw that the spell which had been on us both at that time in Venice had been nothing but the spell and tremendous incantation of the Thought of Death. The dreary city with its decaying palaces and great tomb-encumbered churches had really seemed, in those dark and desolate weeks, to be the home and metropolis of the King of Terrors; and the services at dawn and twilight, with their prayers for the Dead, and funereal candles, had been the chanted ritual of his worship. Now suppose (such was the notion that held my imagination) suppose this spell, which I had felt but for a time and dimly, should become to someone a real obsession, casting its shadow more and more completely over a life otherwise prosperous and happy, might not this be the clue to a history like that of Sir Eustace Carr's – not only his interest in the buried East, his presence at that time in Venice, but also his unexplained and mysterious end?

Musing on this half-believed notion, I thought of the great personages and great nations we read of in ancient history, who have seemed to live with a kind of morbid pleasure in the shadow of this great Thought; who have surrounded themselves with mementoes of Death, and hideous symbols of its power, and who, like the Egyptians, have found their main interest, not in the present, but in imaginary explorations of the unknown future; not on the sunlit surface of this earth, but in the vaults and dwelling-places of the Dead beneath it.

Since this preoccupation, this curiosity, this nostalgia, has exercised so enormous a fascination in the past, I found it not impossible to imagine some modern favourite of fortune falling a victim to this malady of the soul; until at last, growing weary of other satisfactions, he might be drawn to open for himself the dark portal and join the inhabitants of that dim region. This, as I say, was the notion that haunted me, the link my imagination forged between Sir Eustace Carr's presence in that dark Venetian church, and his death some years later. But whether it is really a clue to that unexplained mystery, or whether it is nothing more than a somewhat sinister fancy, of course I cannot say.

Waxworks

'But one really never knows the Age one lives in. How interesting it would be,' I said to the lady next me, 'how I wish we could see ourselves as Posterity will see us!'

I have said it before; but on this occasion I was struck – almost thunder-struck – by my own remark. Like a rash exorcist, I was appalled by the spirit I had raised. For a queer second I did see us all in that inevitable mirror, but cadaverous, palsied, out-of-date – a dusty set of old waxworks, simpering in the lumber-room of Time inanely.

'Better to be forgotten at once!' I exclaimed, with an emphasis that seemed somewhat to surprise the lady next me.

A grievance

They are all persons of elegant manners and spotless reputations; they seem to welcome my visits, and they listen to my anecdotes with unflinching attention. I have only one grievance against them; they will keep in their houses books full of stale epithets, which, when I only seem to smell their mawkish proximity, produce in me a slight feeling of nausea.

There are people, I believe, who are affected in this way by the presence of cats.

The hour-glass

At the corner of Oakley Street I stopped for a moment's chat with my neighbour, Mrs Wheble, who was waiting there for a bus.

'Do tell me,' she asked, 'what you have got in that odd looking parcel?'

'It's an hour-glass,' I said, taking it out of its paper wrapping. 'I've always wanted an hour-glass to measure time by. What a mystery Time really is, when you think of it! See, the sands are running out now while we are talking. I've got here in my hand the most potent, the most enigmatic, the most fleeting of all essences. Time, the sad cure of all our sorrows; but I say! There's your bus just starting. You'll miss it if you don't look out!'

Waiting

We met at Waterloo; as we were paying the same visit, we travelled in the train together; but when we got out at that country station, she found that her boxes had not arrived. They might have gone on to the next station; I waited with her while inquiries were telephoned down the line. It was a mild spring evening: side by side we sat in silence on a wooden bench facing the platform; the bustle caused by the passing train ebbed away; the dusk deepened, and one by one the stars twinkled out in the serene sky.

'How peaceful it is!' I said. 'Is there not a certain charm,' I went on after another pause, 'in waiting like this in silence under the stars? It's after all a little adventure, is it not? a moment with a certain mood and colour and atmosphere of its own.'

'I often think,' I once more mused aloud, 'I often think that it is in moments like this of waiting and hushed suspense that one tastes most fully the savour of life, the uncertainty, and yet the sweetness of our frail mortal condition, so capable of fear and hope, so dependent on a million accidents.'

'Luggage!' I said, after another silence, 'is it not after all absurd that minds that voyage through strange seas should carry about with them brushes and drapery in leather boxes? Suppose all this paltry junk,' I said, giving my suit-case a poke with my umbrella, 'Suppose all this junk should disappear, what after all would it matter?'

At last she spoke. 'But it's my luggage,' she said, 'which is lost.'

Ebury Street

'Do you mean to cut me? How odd you look! What are you doing in Ebury Street?' she asked.

I felt a large, healthy blush suffuse my features. 'There's a lady who lives here – no, I don't mean what you think – a lady,' I said desperately, 'a Mrs Whigham, who hates the way I write, and threw my last book out of her window. I walk by her house now and then to practise humility, and learn – as we all should learn – to endure the world's contempt.'

This Mrs Whigham was, however, an invented being; I had really come to Ebury Street for another look, in the window of a shop there, at an old Venetian mirror, in whose depths of dusky glass I had seen a dim, romantic, well-dressed figure, as I went by one day.

The bubble

Walking home at night, troubled by the world's affairs, and with its weight of Wrong crushing down my poor shoulders, I sometimes allow my Thoughts an interlude of solace. From the jar in which I keep my Vanity bottled, I remove the cork; out rushes that friendly Jinn and swells up and fills the sky. I walk on lightly through another world, a world in which I cut a very different figure.

I shall not describe that exquisite, evanescent universe; I soon snuff it out, or it melts of itself in thin air.

At the club

'It's the result of Board School Education——'
   'It's the popular Press——'
   'It's the selfishness of the Working Classes——'
   'It's the Cinema——'
   'It's the Jews——'
   'Paid Agitators!——'
   'The decay of Faith——'
   'The disintegration of Family Life——'
   'I put it down,' I said, 'to Sun-spots. If you want to know,' I went inexorably on, 'if you ask me the cause of all this modern Unrest——'

Eclipse

A mild radiance and the scent of flowers filled the drawing-room, whose windows stood open to the summer night. I thought our talk delightful; the topic was one of my favourite topics; I had much that was illuminating to say about it, and I was a little put out when we were called to the window to look at the planet Jupiter, which was shining in the sky just then, we were told, with great brilliance.

In turns through a telescope we gazed at the Planet. I thought the spectacle over-rated. However I said nothing. Not for the world, not for any number of worlds would I have wished them to guess why I was displeased with that star.

Achievement

'Yes, as you say, one certainly ought to try to make something of one's life. It's an experience after all, full of exasperation of course, but full of interest. And love, and the warmth of the sun are pleasant, and money, and the taste of food. And how pleasant it is, too, to shine in conversation!'

'What I think would be perfectly charming,' I confided to our Vicar's wife, 'what above all things I should like, would be to make out of my life – how shall I put it? – something delicate and durable, something privileged to win the approbation of the high authorities of the Universe. To live on, in fact, after my funeral in a perfect phrase.'

3. from

Last Words (1933)

Growing old is no gradual decline, but a series of falls, full of sorrow, from one ledge to another. Yet when we pick ourselves up we find that our bones are not broken; while not unpleasing is the new terrace which lies unexplored before us.

Oh dear, this living and eating and growing old; these doubts and aches in the back, and want of interest in Nightingales and Roses . . .

Am I the person who used to wake in the middle of the night and laugh with the joy of living? Who worried about the existence of God, and danced with young ladies till long after daybreak? Who sang 'Auld Lang Syne' and howled with sentiment, and more than once gazed at the full moon through a blur of great, romantic tears?

How can they say my life is not a success? Have I not for more than sixty years got enough to eat and escaped being eaten?

I got up with Stoic fortitude of mind in the cold this morning; but afterwards, in my hot bath, I joined the school of Epicurus. I was a Materialist at breakfast; after it an Idealist, as I smoked my first cigarette and turned the world to transcendental vapour. But when I began to read *The Times* I had no doubt of the existence of an external world.

So all the morning and all the afternoon opinions kept flowing into and out of the receptacle of my mind; till by the time the enormous day was over, it had been filled by most of the widely-known Theories of Existence, and emptied of them.

This long speculation of life, this thinking and syllogizing that always goes on inside me, this running over and over of hypothesis and surmise and supposition – one day this infinite Argument will have ended, the debate will be for ever over, I shall have come to an indisputable conclusion, and my brain will be at rest.

4. *Epilogue* from

All Trivia (1933)

Epilogue

'What funny coats you wear, dear Readers! And your hats! The thought of your hats does make me laugh.'

Thus across the great gulf of Time I send, with a wave of my hand, a greeting to that quaint people we call Posterity, whom I, like other great writers, claim as my readers, – urging them to hurry up and get born, that they may have the pleasure of reading TRIVIA.